TATTING TECHNIQUES

Old Revivals and New Experiments

By the same author:

A NEW LOOK IN TATTING (Alec Tiranti—now available from Academy Editions, London)

HANDBOOK OF TATTING (Vista Books—out of print but may be found in libraries)

TATTING TECHNIQUES

Old Revivals and New Experiments

Elgiva Nicholls

CHARLES SCRIBNER'S SONS
New York

1 3 5 7 9 11 13 15 17 19 I/C 20 18 16 14 12 10 8 6 4 2

Printed in Great Britain
Library of Congress Catalog Card Number 75–29906
ISBN 0–684–14591–X

Contents

List of Plates

of completed work by the author

Part 1

BASIC PRINCIPLES

DEFINITION

Tatting is a form of the very old craft of knotting, which was evolved in prehistoric times. There are a surprising number of knots, useful and ornamental. Some 7,000 have been recorded in *Ashley's Book of Knots,* each designed for a particular purpose. Real lace, the manufacture of which is a sophisticated art, is composed of many kinds of ornamental knots and stitches, of which the tatting knot is one. Originally (and currently) used in seamanship, it has for some long time now been accepted as decorative, and since it can produce lace by itself though of a rudimentary kind, the result can be described as true lace, humble, but with a distinguished ancestry. This distinction is important, because it separates tatting from crochet and knitting. 'Laces' produced by these methods are 'bastard' laces—much younger imitations. They are not in the same class, and cannot be compared with tatting. They are highly developed crafts, but with a different origin and history.

THE TATTING KNOT

The tatting knot is a double knot, composed of two half-hitches, one the mirror image of the other, carried on another and independent thread, which forms an internal core; hence the strength and comparative firmness of the work.

Construction of The Lark's Head

You will be able to make the knot more easily, if you understand how it is composed, and its peculiar property, which is shown in the following demonstration. Take two pieces of supple cord, of contrasting colours, say black and white, each about 18 inches in length, and with the fingers compose the knot, very loosely, following the drawing Fig. I. 1a. Arranged thus, this double knot is technically 'A Lark's Head on a running line'. These are knotting terms and are not part of tatting vocabulary, which would describe it as 'A double-stitch on the shuttle thread'. 'Running Line' is more expressive and is used throughout this book.

If the two free ends of the white cord forming the knot are pulled sharply apart, while the (shaded) cord is completely relaxed, a transformation results: the shaded cord now forms the knots, and the white cord has become the running line, shown in Fig. I. 1b. You have, in knotting parlance,

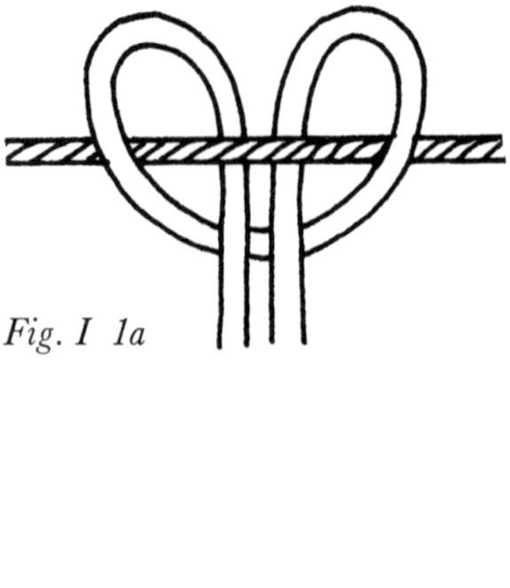

Fig. I 1a

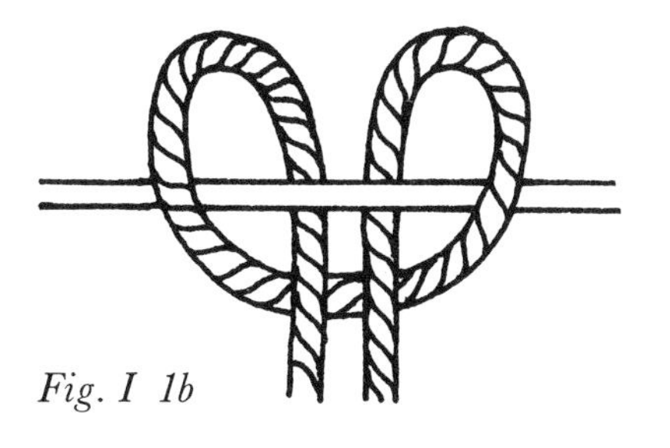
Fig. I 1b

capsized the knot: the function of the cords has been exchanged. (The action is reversible.) This apparent sleight of hand takes place in the action of tatting. Every half-hitch (or single stitch) is made first with one thread, and then capsized or turned to reappear on the other, the foundation thread always running clear, and supporting the knots, or as the pair are called, the Double Stitch. It is not really a stitch, as stitches are made with needles, but it is described as a stitch in all languages.

In the actual work of making rings and chains, the Lark's Head is turned round so that the free ends of the thread and the stitches face upwards or outwards, away from you, but for demonstration of the action it is clearer to show it as drawn. All tatting is composed of this knot only. Variations in appearance are brought about by making a number of small adjustments, but the knot remains essentially the same.

Before actually making the knot with a thread carried on the shuttle, it is important to consider the properties necessary in the thread used, and its thickness.

MATERIALS

Theoretically you can tat with a hair or a thick rope. Calibre makes no difference, except in the resultant size of the work. For example, 50 double stitches to the inch, or 8 doubles in the space of one inch. Something in between is preferable. Whatever the material, it must be smooth, pliable yet firm, tightly twisted, with as little 'stretch' as possible. Cotton is the most practicable, hence its universal use, but other threads can be used: these are suggested later for more advanced work.

While still supporting the traditional school, I have felt it necessary to follow the times, as do other writers, and design for bolder work. Delicacy may not have been the main object, but strong clean lines and well placed ornament also have something to contribute to a finished piece. For this, thicker thread is better.

Most of the illustrations here are worked in cotton No. 20, which is coarse. Start using 20 to learn the stitch, and move on perhaps to 60, which is a good average size. If however you are interested in fine work only, start straight off with 70 and possibly progress to 100: for simple edgings this is not as difficult as it sounds. Whatever pattern you undertake, you are not obliged to use the thickness recommended: you can use thicker or finer, whichever suits you best. The only difference will be the size of the finished piece; it will be larger, or smaller, than the given measurements. It may not suit the design so well, but it is still workable.

THE SHUTTLE

The shuttle is a convenient holder of thread and no more. Its size makes no difference to the size of the work which depends only on the thread. Neither does it make the stitch for you; this is formed by movement of the fingers.

Winding the shuttle

To thread or wind, pass the end of the thread through the hole in the centre block, and knot it, cutting off the free end. Wind the thread evenly: if the shuttle is filled to capacity, no thread should protrude past the edges of the blades. An overloaded shuttle causes the blade tips to be forced apart and strains them. If by mistake the thread becomes caught over the face of one of the blades, unwind back to this point and rewind.

Holding the shuttle

The active or working shuttle is held in the right hand like a pencil, blade uppermost. It has no back or front, being the same at both ends, until it is held in the hand: then the end approaching the left hand is referred to as the front. The thread should leave the shuttle from the side furthest away from you, at the back. You will be passing the shuttle over and under a taut thread held in the left hand. The shuttle must be held firmly but lightly enough so that the thread, whether above or below the blade, slips smoothly between it and the fingers (above) or thumb (below). Hence the necessity for leaving the blade clear of loose ends or threads caught across them through careless winding.

A PRACTICE CHAIN

Most tatting books give instructions for making the ring first and the chain second. Historically the ring came long before the chain. The stitch of course is the same in both, the shuttle thread forming the running line: in the ring, only one thread is used, a distant part of itself forming the stitches. In the chain, the stitches are made of an independent second thread, also described as the auxiliary thread, either attached to the ball, or wound on a second shuttle for convenience. Where there are two threads they may be of different colours, e.g. black and white, so that the transference of the knot may be more clearly seen, an advantage to beginners. We therefore start with a chain of two threads, black in the shuttle, white for the ball, which will make the knots.

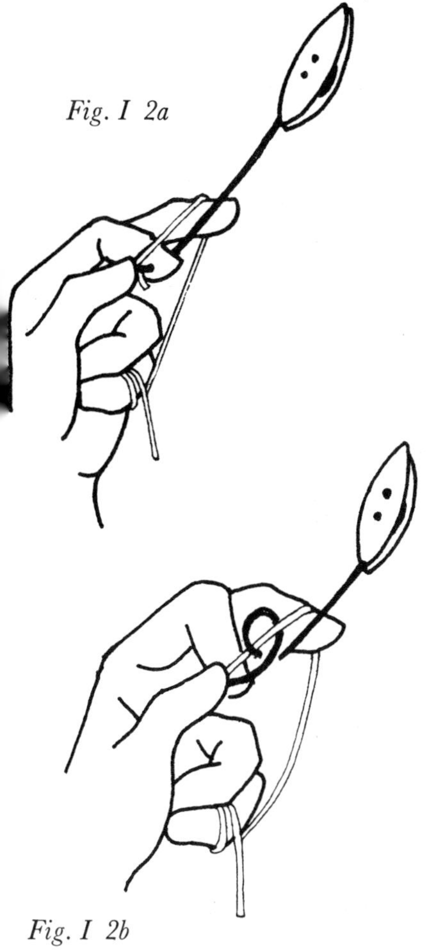

Fig. I 2a

Fig. I 2b

To make a chain with threads of two colours

To the free end of the shuttle thread (black) tie a length of white (about one yard for practice, or work direct from the ball) with a reef knot. Hold this knot between the first finger and thumb of the left hand, the black thread nearest to you. Pass the white thread behind the slightly extended middle finger and twist it two or three times round the little finger to steady it. You will now have a taut white line about two inches in length between the reef knot hidden under the thumb and the middle finger, shown in Fig. I. 2a. This is the section upon which the knot will be made.

By extending or relaxing the middle finger the thread can be tightened or slackened as required. The left hand is now ready for work. Hold the shuttle, as previously described, about 8 inches away from the reef knot and pass the thread behind the little finger of the right hand to steady it.

The first half of the double stitch

Bring the shuttle up to the left hand and slip it under the two threads (its own thread and the taut section) as if you were lifting them, sliding it through smoothly, the two threads slipping between the shuttle and the first finger. This is awkward at first but this method enables you to work at speed eventually. When the back end of the shuttle is just clear of the two threads, bring it back again without turning it round, but this time *over* the white thread and *under* the black, so that a black knot is formed about an inch away from the thumb. Fig. I. 2b shows this.

If much closer than an inch, it will not have room to turn. Do not hold the shuttle up in the air—this will make the knot come too near. Now turn it with a very slight jerking or flipping movement, at the same time relaxing the taut thread, by letting the middle finger drop, and tightening the shuttle thread by slipping it clear of the little finger. The knot will be transferred to it, becoming a white one lying on the black. The presence of the black knot is momentary. When you are working smoothly you will not be conscious of it and you will never see it, as it will form and turn automatically, virtually in one movement. If it refuses to turn with your first efforts, it is because (*a*) it is too close in to the thumb or (*b*) the taut thread is not sufficiently relaxed. In the words of the author of a little booklet entitled *Album for Frivolity Works*, date circa 1845: 'The persons neglecting that recommendation would immediately see the knots formed by the independent thread, and thereby be in the absolute impossibility of continuing the work.' Just so, because the running thread is caught, by a stitch of its own making. Keep on trying: some beginners take a long time to perform the turn. Then, suddenly, it appears. When it does, it is a moment of triumph.

Tilt the knot hard up against the reef knot—the start of the chain. For practice make several, until you are sure of the movement. All the knots must be white: if one is black you have not turned it and the chain will not pull up. If you make half a dozen or more, with some cottons the chain will begin to twist on itself. This is natural, because the stitches are all of one kind, all pulling in the same direction. The second half of the stitch, when following the first, will counteract this. Learn the second as soon as you have mastered the first: it is slightly simpler. At first your knots will probably be very loose. They will get tighter as you improve, by extending the middle finger for each one made, thus drawing away surplus thread.

The second half of the double stitch

Bring the shuttle up as before, but carry it beyond and *over* the taut thread (letting it balance on the middle finger) and returning under it, and then over its own threads, pressing the thread downwards with the right thumb to give you more room. Turn the knot as before. It is the first one in reverse. Fig. I. 2c shows the two, turned, namely the complete double stitch.

In the drawing of the Lark's Head, the stitches were shown loose: here each of course must be tightened as soon as made, and pushed back into position under the thumb. Continue making doubles, and as you progress move the left finger and thumb forward along the chain so that you have more control.

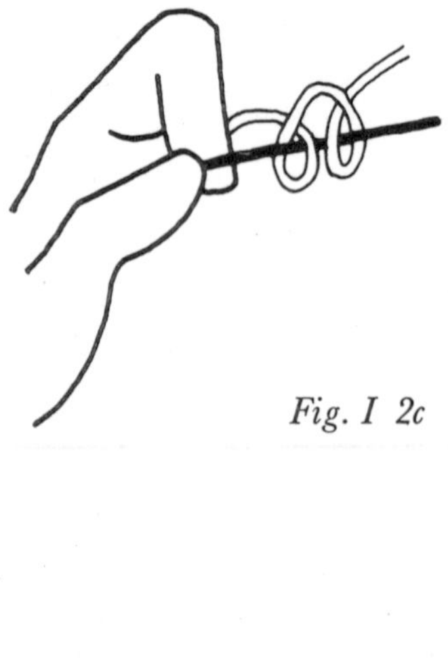

Fig. I 2c

The chain you have made is a practice piece—to learn the stitch, assisted by the use of two colours. You now need to make one of one thread, as the ring is, the knots (as in the ring) being formed by a distant part of itself. This is not usually taught in English patterns, but it is routine in most foreign books. It was in fact used by early English workers, but has dropped out of common practice. To avoid an unnecessary join is one of the objects of good design. This technique, described as the continuous thread method, dispenses with one.

To start a chain on a continuous thread

Wind the shuttle, but do not cut off the ball. Unwind as much as you need from the ball, now cut it off and wind back the thread on a second shuttle until the two meet, about 12 inches apart. You can, if preferred, work direct from the ball, it depends on the length of thread that you need, but the second shuttle, if justified, keeps the thread under better control.

With the 'stretch of thread' between the two shuttles, form a hairpin bend, holding the bend under the left thumb, the first shuttle thread nearest to you, the second beyond it, arranging the thread round the hand as you did the white thread in the practice chain. Make four or five doubles in the usual way. There is no reef knot under the thumb, so keep the stitches out where you can see them. Now let go the left hand, disclosing the bend at the head. Holding the stitches, pull the first shuttle firmly but carefully until the loop has completely telescoped into the chain, giving a blind end. Continue working for as long as you need. The work cannot come undone, as there is no join, and there is no preliminary holding knot, as was formerly made in a chain of this type, which made a comparatively clumsy start. For practice pieces, it is not necessary to use the second shuttle. Leave about a yard of free thread from the first shuttle before making the bend, and work on this.

Beginners' pieces seldom, if ever, start with a chain, but many advanced patterns do, and it is as well to learn it now.

A chain following a ring, without adding a new thread

An occasion when you will be using it frequently is in a pattern starting with a ring, followed by a chain. The usual instructions are to tie the ball thread to the base of the ring, thus leaving two free ends. These are avoided by using the continuous thread, which provides the auxiliary already in position: no join is needed. To follow with the chain, turn the work over, as chains are usually worked on the reverse side. As you have not yet learnt the ring, you cannot at present practise this, but you soon will.

TO MAKE A RING

The knots of course are made in the same way as in the chain, but the single thread is held in a slightly different manner.

Lay the shuttle thread across the palm of the left hand, the free end (about 6 inches) towards you, and hold it firmly between the first finger and thumb—this will be the starting point. Carry the thread over the middle finger, extending the finger to leave about two inches of taut thread between it and the thumb. Take the thread on behind the third finger and up to the starting point, and hold it there. You now have a triangle of thread held in shape by three fingers: this triangle becomes the ring when a sufficient number of stitches are worked on it, and surplus thread withdrawn. Before you attempt to make the stitch, stretch the second and third fingers, still gripping the two threads under the thumb, but allowing the shuttle thread to move freely, so that the triangle can be made larger: make it smaller by pulling on the shuttle, which is a pull in the opposite direction. Do this several times until you can control its size, and are familiar with the action. Fig. I. 3a shows the triangle in position, ready for the stitch.

Fig. I 3a

As you already know how to make the stitch, the instructions are not repeated, and a drawing should not be necessary. Make the first half, and slide it back to be held under the thumb: make the second half, and settle it close to the first. As you do not now have the two colours to guide you, make sure that the stitches are correctly turned: test every one before making the next by ensuring that the running line is free and clear. Do this by pulling on the shuttle. If it will not move, one of the stitches is at fault. The triangle will become smaller with every stitch made, as it is being used up to make them. Keep it a convenient size. Too small, and you will not have room to turn the stitches. To enlarge it, pull (with the finger and thumb of the right hand) the triangle thread at the start of the ring. Aim at a large triangle and a short shuttle thread. Work at least twelve doubles and then close the ring by disengaging the hands, and, holding the stitches carefully, pull on the shuttle thread until all the excess is drawn away, and start and finish meet. For practice make a number of rings of different sizes, one following the other on the same thread.

TENSION OF BOTH THREADS

Before describing the picot and the join, which both rings and chain can feature, take a look at those which you have already worked. Good tatting is tight, even, and lies flat. These qualities are acquired by correct tension, which only comes with practice. When making the stitch, you are concerned with two threads (in a ring as well). The tension of both must be under control, or you will not get the desired effect.

The running thread

In the chain a slight curve is natural. This is because the stitches carry more thread on the outer edge: they take up more room on this side than the other. The tighter the running thread the steeper the curve, and the chain shortens. Both are correct: it depends on the effect you want. Rather surprisingly, if the thread is *very* slack, but the stitches tight, the chain will curve in the opposite direction—a phenomenon to be exploited later.

In the ring, normal tension produces a pear-shape. Slightly tighter, and it will become round. Slacker, and you can produce a long narrow one. To get these two effects, press into position with the fingers.

The thread forming the stitches

In both ring and chain, too slack a tension will produce uneven work, and possibly unwanted picots. If really tight, you cannot draw up a large ring: the stitches strangle it. Therefore correct tension of both threads is essential. Attention to it at the very beginning will save a good deal of trouble, for if at fault, the finished result will not turn out to be the size or shape you expected.

THE PICOT

A picot is formed by making a double stitch the required distance away from the stitch before it, that is by making the first half and turning it, but not sliding it up until the second half locks it into position. When drawn up, the picot will be half the length of the measured distance. A ring cannot start with a picot, neither can it end with one, since a double stitch is required to precede and make it.

Normally, the length of the picot is judged by eye, as they are reasonably short. More advanced work uses them in many sizes: methods of measuring them are given later.

The picot is primarily an ornament, but also a joining agent. A join is effected by integrating it into the work, that is joining a second ring, while under construction, to the first. This method, arrived at after much early experiment, and now universal, is described.

THE JOIN TO A PICOT

A ring can join to a picot at any point in its construction. During the making of a second ring, when ready to join, sufficient thread from the triangle is pulled as a loop from underneath through the picot with a small steel hook. The loop must be large enough to pass the shuttle through it. Then pull the shuttle thread gently, at the same time extending the middle finger (left hand) so pulling on the loop until its tip lies close up against the stitch just worked: all that remains of it is the tip, resting on the picot, which must be tight up against the running thread. This drawn-through loop takes up space, and so counts as the first half of a double stitch. Now work the second half. The pair counts as a double, belonging to and counted in the section between the join and the next picot. Practise by making a ring with several picots, well spaced, and joining into them with other rings. If the join is well made, you will hardly be able to distinguish which ring is carrying the picot. Fig. I. 4a shows the loop ready to receive the shuttle.

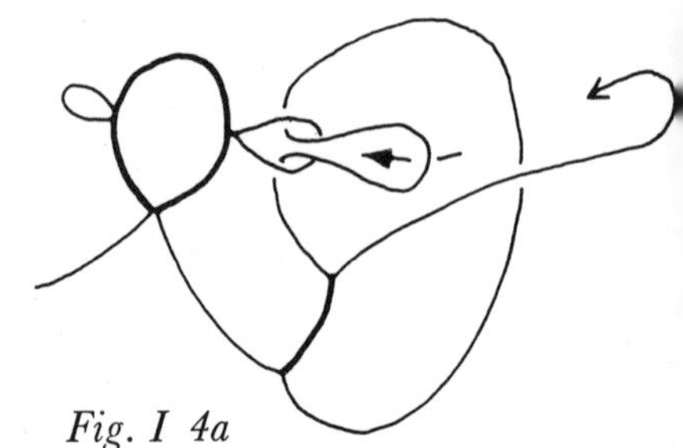

Fig. I 4a

Chains of course can join to picots on rings in the same manner, provided the auxiliary thread is nearest to the ring. If it is on the opposite or 'off' side, the running thread instead has to be drawn through the picot and knotted into it. This needs careful adjustment because the knot breaks the tension of the chain. More about this join is given later.

THE PATTERN

Classical tatting patterns are built up of lines and circles, the most basic of all shapes. Arrangements of these two are infinite, and a catalogue of them would never be complete. A great many, however, have been recorded, so that they can be preserved and repeated. The record is the pattern.

A pattern gives information on how to produce the effect required. It should be clear and concise, leaving no doubt as to its intention. This is difficult to achieve in any language, hence the necessity of so many pictorial aids to interpret them. After a study of foreign patterns, the English system of writing would seem to reach this ideal as well as any, for it leaves less to chance and misinterpretation than most others, which often depend too much on illustrations of one style or another, sometimes too small to follow. Nevertheless, I would like to reconsider the present system of writing and illustrating, and possibly make some alterations to it. That they are improvements is of course a matter of opinion.

Presentation of the pattern

Tatting patterns, since they are all composed of rings and/or chains, appear on reading to be remarkably similar. It would be easier, both for the beginner and the experienced worker, if some method were used which gave in addition to the bare working instructions, some preliminary account or description of the nature of the design. Without it, it is almost impossible to visualise the intended result. This would at least give it an identity, and the directions to follow would then be more comprehensible. For convenience in working, the pattern can be divided into two parts, the preliminary description and the construction, with a working formula of each ring and chain, accompanied if necessary by a diagram which would illustrate beyond doubt any particular passages.

The preliminary description

This is intended to give a brief overall description of the piece, which is usually composed of an orderly assembly of rings and chains forming a unit. We are at present referring only to straight edgings, in which the unit is presumed to be repeated indefinitely: in a circular piece it is limited to a given number. This is described later in the paragraph on medallions. The composition of the unit—say three rings and two chains—should be stated, and any special features as shown in Part II. With this advance information you have a clearer idea of the scope of the piece, and *what* you are going to do, before you actually start on it. The description should be checked with the illustration, which will familiarise you with its component parts, and their position.

Construction, formula and diagram

Explanatory notes tell you *how* you are going to do it. The order of work is given, and the point at which the work starts. This may seem superfluous, as its position no doubt comes naturally to most workers, but to many beginners it does not, and they feel they are expected to embark on what appears to them to be an uncharted maze of directions from an unidentified point. So often the opening word in a pattern is '1st ring'. . . . Ring? which ring? . . . it's nothing *but* rings!

Working instructions—the number of stitches and the position of picots and joins are condensed into a formula. What cannot be shown in this is covered in the notes. Current tatting patterns are virtually written as formulae but some modifications are here suggested. Where any part of the pattern has to be repeated, e.g. part of a ring, or a whole repetition, that part can be enclosed in brackets, preceded by the appropriate number, as in arithmetic. Further, I feel that the standard term 'close the ring' could be omitted. If the total number of doubles—in addition to the bare formula—is supplied as an extra check, you should know when to close it.

This form of presentation may be over-complicated for very simple pieces, but for the more elaborate it is an advantage to follow a system which defines and separates the various aspects of the work.

The diagram is difficult to stylise. A single line has to represent two conditions—unworked thread and a row of stitches, as required. Actually to depict the stitches would produce a drawing, which should be in correct proportion, but we are composing a diagram, which purposely is not. It must be as simple as possible and easy to reproduce in print, with no confusing pictorial details. As to the picot and its representation I do not like picots drawn in as actual loops. If a single line can represent them (as in German patterns) the effect is simpler and better. The picots therefore are shown as short single strokes carried on the ring. A stroke to which a new ring joins is carried on for a short distance inside it. This is logical because, as explained in the making of the join, the picot tip is carried on the new running thread. You also see which is passive (the existing picot) and which is active (the new ring). The single stroke is, however, not always practicable: sometimes to draw a loop makes the diagram clearer.

Picots can be spaced so that one follows another immediately. There will then be one double between each, *the one in fact which forms them.* These I call 'adjoining' picots. With two doubles between them I call them 'two doubles apart', and so on. Most English patterns describe this as 'separated by one double' (or by two doubles, as the case may be). This has the same result but is differently expressed.

Some simple pieces written as formulae, and illustrated with diagrams

Abbreviations: R =Ring: Ch =Chain: P =Picot: J, =Join: ds =double stitch

A comma after the J prevents its confusion with ensuing figures. Here are two rings. The first carries a picot at its apex.

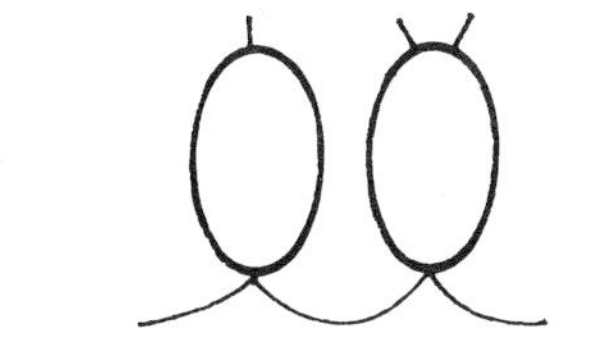

Fig. I 5a

Formula: 8ds P 8ds. (Total 16 doubles).
The second carries two picots, two doubles apart.

Formula: 7ds P 2ds P 7ds. (Total 16ds). A row of single rings makes the simplest of all edgings—no joins. The two rings are shown in the diagram Fig. I. 5a.
Here is a row of similar rings, carrying one ornamental picot at the apex, and one on either side for joining.

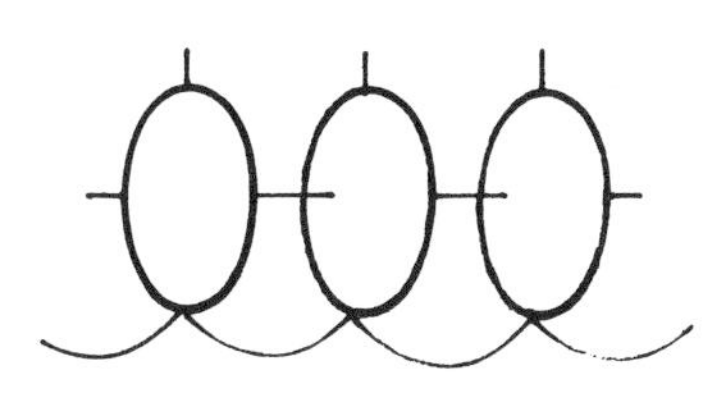

Fig. I 6a

Formula: 1st ring: 4ds 3(P 4ds). 2nd ring: 4ds J, 2 (4ds P) 4ds. Make the first ring: follow with the second: all ensuing rings as second. Shown in the diagram Fig. I. 6a.
Patterns often contain the abbreviation RV, indicating that for the next portion the piece has to be reversed, for tatting is not always worked with the same side uppermost.

Reversing the work: This is done to avoid the crossing of threads, which theoretically should never happen. The auxiliary should lie above, the shuttle thread below, at all times. If a ring has to lie in a new position, crossing would occur in certain formations unless reversing takes place. In a piece all composed of rings, where one faces up, the following one down, the work is reversed after each ring, so that the thread leaving it is always in the correct position for the next. If you could make alternate rings with the left hand holding the shuttle, reversing would not be necessary. The thread would emerge from the correct side. As this is unlikely, the instruction to reverse is given.

Here is a construction you will meet very often. It is a double row of rings, worked alternately up and down. In both upper and lower rows, each joins to its neighbour. The formula is the same for all, except for the first two rings which have nothing to join to, and therefore carry picots only. They all consist of 24ds.

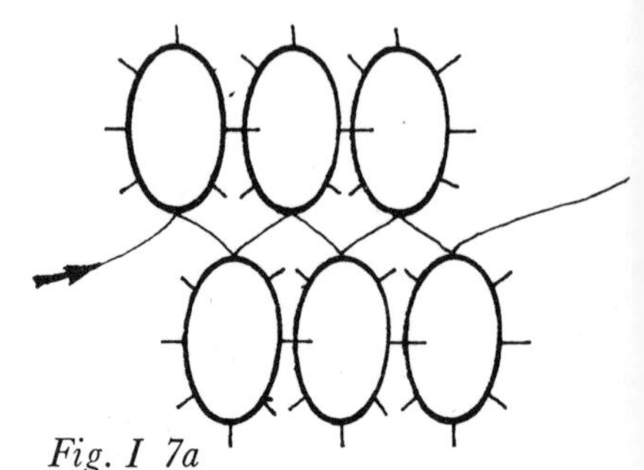

Fig. I 7a

The first two rings, upper and lower left: 7(3ds P) 3ds. RV.

All others, upper and lower: 3ds P 3ds J, 5(3ds P) 3ds. RV. They are shown in the diagram Fig. I. 7a.

The last example involves an ornamented chain, alternating with rings which are unjoined.

R: 4ds 3(P 4ds). RV.

Ch: 3(3ds P) 3ds. RV.

Work the ring first on a continuous thread, and follow with the chain. By reversing after the ring the threads will be ready for the chain, which will face down. Reverse again ready for the next ring. Shown in the diagram Fig. I. 8a.

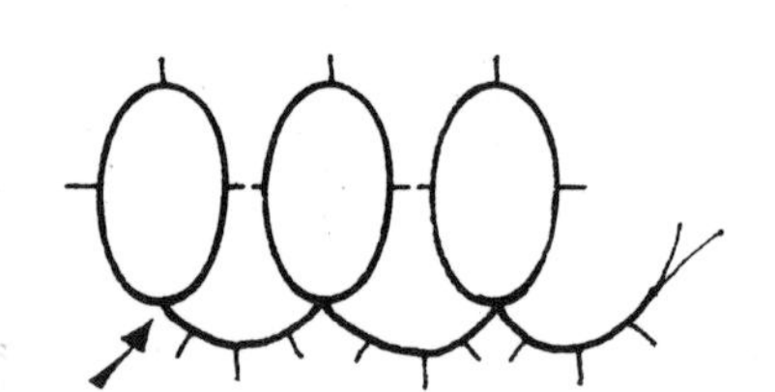

Fig. I 8a

Having been introduced to the rudiments of an edging, and the method of describing it, look closely at edgings in other pattern books. Study the position of the rings, which may vary: they may face up, down, or sideways. Work some strips of rings of different sizes: they are very good practice. Edgings, which may consist of several rows, or rounds, are of great interest to some workers, as if they are applied to handkerchiefs, where at the corners two lines meet at right angles, the pattern needs modification, a challenge to the designer. A very simple row of rings without joins can be eased round a corner without alteration, but rings that are joined need special adjustment to fit.

A COLLECTION OF EDGINGS

The following six patterns are by no means elementary. They are chosen to demonstrate how rings, alone or with chains, can show a great variety of form by simply placing them in different combinations. Their description is briefer than for the previous 'patterns'. If you are really a beginner, study them, otherwise turn straight to the section on medallions (p. 31).

Daisy Chain

This is a row of ornamented rings carrying six picots two doubles apart. Each successive ring joins to the last picot but one of the ring before it. The picots are rather large, and a long space of thread lies between each ring. In the model it is a measured $\frac{3}{4}$ inch, but this is a matter of choice. In finer thread it would of course be less. It can be eased round a corner and is very attractive on a fine lawn handkerchief. The spacing threads are attached to the fabric.

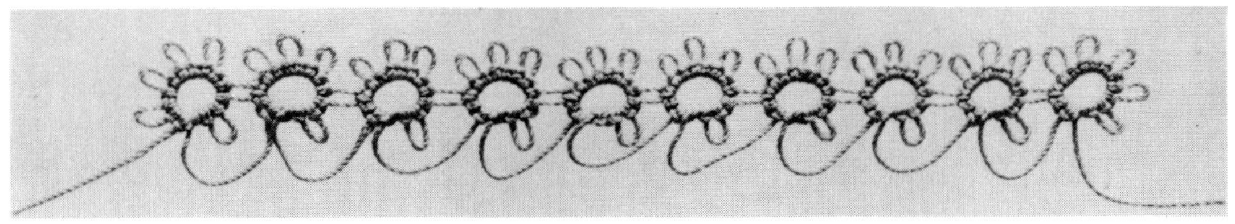

Fig. I 9

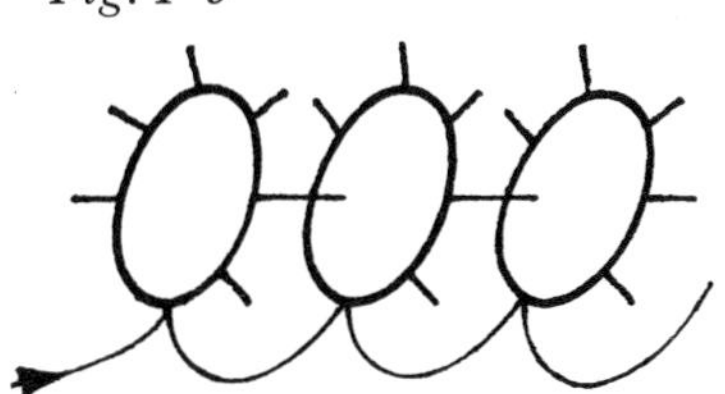

Fig. I 9a

Formula:
1st ring: 6(2ds P) 2ds
2nd ring: 2ds J, 5(2ds P) 2ds.
All succeeding rings are as the second. If the last ring is to join into the first, instead of making the fifth picot, join into the first picot of the first ring. The model is shown in Fig. 1. 9, its diagram in Fig. 1. 9a.

Diamonds

This is composed of individually worked units (the diamonds) each on a new thread. It is more in the nature of a trimming, arranged as an edging, which as a rule is worked as a whole without a break.

A diamond: four identical rings facing outwards are drawn into a circle. They carry ornamental picots and are joined to one another.

Formula: 1st ring: 5ds P 4ds 4(P 2ds) P 4ds P 5ds. (Total 26ds). The second and third rings are made in the same manner, but substituting a join for the first picot. The fourth ring joins to the first picot of the first ring. This join is a difficult one as it is an awkward position. It occurs in many medallions. On completion tie the ends and cut off. Work a second diamond in the same manner. It will join to the first.

Any of its rings can perform the join but the last but one is the most convenient. Any ring on the first diamond can receive it.

Formula for the joining ring:

5ds P 4ds P 2ds J, 4ds J, 2ds P 4ds P 5ds.

Notice that there are two joins, and in this ring the centre picot of the usual group of five is omitted as there is not space for it. Three diamonds are shown in the model Fig. I. 10, and the diagram Fig. I. 10a shows the joins between two.

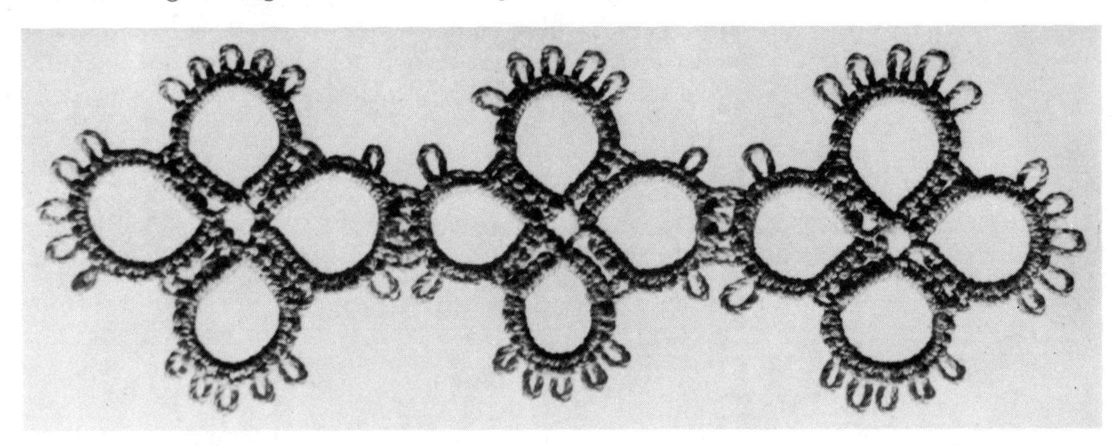

Fig. I 10

Fig. I 10a

Italian Butterfly

Two upper rings at an opposing angle are joined near their bases. Below and between them is a free-standing ornamented ring, facing down, which is the second ring in the formula. The third ring completes the upper pair, the three forming one repetition. In the starting ring of the first repetition a picot is shown after the first eight doubles. In all subsequent first rings, this picot is replaced by a join. The ornamented ring is worked on the reverse side. Check these points with the diagram before beginning to work.

Formula:

1st ring: 8ds P 4ds P 9ds P 3ds. (Total 24ds). RV.
2nd ring: 7(2ds P) 2ds. (Total 16ds). RV.
3rd ring: 3ds J, 9ds P 4ds P 8ds. (Total 24ds).
Work the rings in the above order, and leave a long space of thread (about ½ in. or 1 cm in the model) before beginning the next group.

A corner: This is one normal repetition except that there are three ornamented rings instead of one, close together and joined to one another, the second to the last picot of the first, the third to the last picot of the second. The third (upper) ring follows as usual, then the space of thread. Make sure that the spaces on either side of the corner are long enough, otherwise it cannot lie flat. When sewn to fabric, the two upper rings are pinched tightly together, making them narrower.

The model shows four repetitions on the lower edge, the corner and one repetition following in Fig. I. 11. The diagram, Fig. I. 11a, shows two repetitions on either side of the corner. The distances between the rings are exaggerated to show the joins more clearly. The central enclosure made by the rings at the corner should be small and neat.

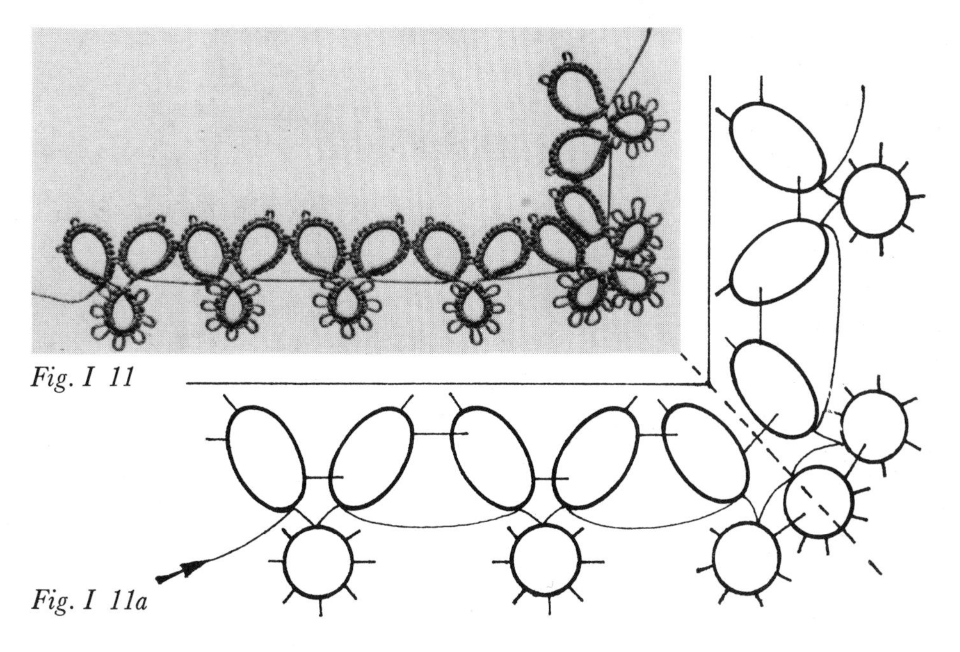

Fig. I 11

Fig. I 11a

Straight Strips

Two identical rings, set opposite one another, and joined at their tips, are connected by a semi-circular chain carrying one picot at its centre, which lies beneath them. This is one repetition. By working with a continuous thread there need be no free ends at the start. Make the first ring, then the chain, then the second ring, following the formula in the order given thus:

1st ring: 10ds P 10ds. (Total 20ds). RV.
Chain: 8ds P 8ds. RV.
2nd ring: 10ds J, 10ds.

To turn a corner: on a new pair of threads link into the picot on a chain and start a new repetition at right angles to the first strip. This is an unorthodox method of working a corner, which is normally achieved without a fresh start, but is possible here because, roughly speaking, the repetition is as broad as it is long. Because this is so, new strips can be started from any of the chains, to build up rectangles of any size.

The model Fig. I. 12 shows a strip of five repetitions and two following at right angles. The diagram, Fig. I. 12a, shows a corner. The piece is given mainly for practice in working rings and chains alternately, drawing up the rings so that they are as nearly as possible the same shape and size, and making a neat junction at the bases of the rings and the start and finish of chains, which all meet at one point.

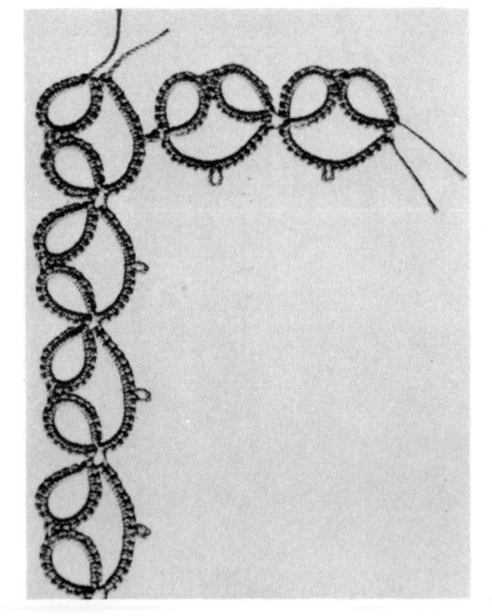

Fig. I 12

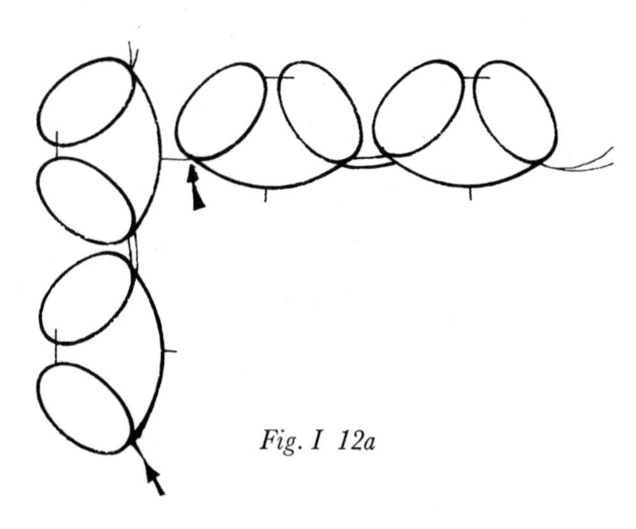

Fig. I 12a

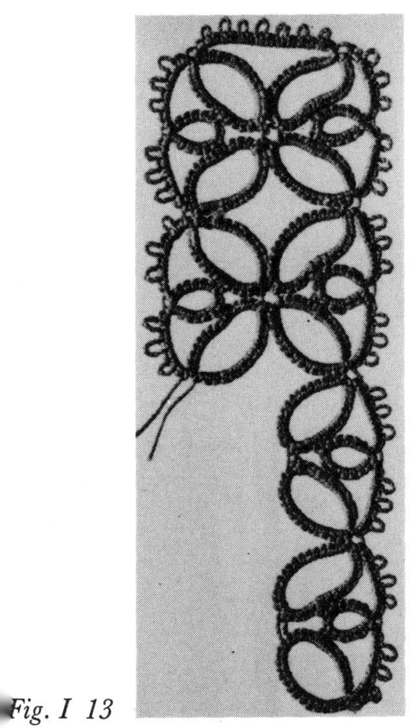

Fig. I 13

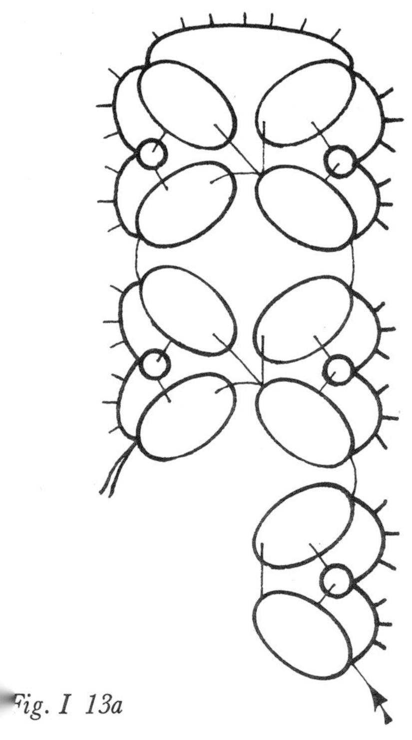

Fig. I 13a

Spanish Insertion

This consists of a straight strip, rather similar to the previous one, but more elaborate. It can be used alone, or with another similar strip added to it, worked back to lie opposite the first, to which it joins. A double edging of this kind forms an insertion—both sides alike. The model shows both the single and double form.

Formula:

1st ring: (large): 15ds P 5ds P 10ds. (Total 30ds). RV.
1st chain: 3(2ds P) 2ds. RV.
2nd ring: (small): 6ds J, 3ds P 6ds. (Total 17ds). RV.
2nd chain: as first. RV.
3rd ring: (large): 10ds J, 5ds J, 15ds.
The last join of the third ring is to the first picot of the first ring, as the diagram shows. Work in the order given. In the second round, if added, the first large ring does not carry the first picot, since it joins directly (as does also the third ring) into the picot carried on the first round. Therefore make this picot rather larger as there will be altogether three joins into it. If too small the four large rings will be dragged out of shape. There should be a small, clear open centre.

In the model, in order to work both rounds on one pair of threads, an end-piece of a chain carrying seven picots two doubles apart was worked. This is optional. Otherwise, start the second round on a new pair of threads.

The model, Fig. I. 13, shows four repetitions of the lower round, and two of the upper. The diagram, Fig. I. 13a, is the same.

Scallops

This is an edging or border of two rounds. The first is attached to fabric, the second is a series of scallops joined to it.

The first round: This consists of rings joined to one another, alternating with chains, which are sewn on to the fabric. The rings, which will become nearly circular, face away from it.
Ring: 5ds 3(P 5ds). (Total 20ds). RV.
Chain: 5ds P 5ds. RV.
For all successive rings, replace the first picot by a join to the preceding one. Work in the order given, which is one repetition of the first round.

The corner ring: The corner ring, which is slightly larger, follows a normal ring, to which it joins at its first picot position. After the corner ring a new repetition is started, its first ring joining to the corner. These three rings are worked in close succession.

Formula for the corner:
5ds J, 3(5ds P) 5ds.
To work as much as the model shows, work nine repetitions, but omit the last chain: then the corner ring, following with five repetitions, which will lie at right angles to the first section. This completes the first round.

The second round: This also consists of rings alternating with chains, very similar to the first row, but applied to it in the opposite direction, so that the rings face up or inwards, joining to selected rings on the first round. They are arranged to form scallops, each consisting of six rings, three long chains and two short. The formulae for these three units is as follows:
Ring: 7ds J, 5ds P 7ds. (Total 19ds)
Short chain: 8ds only.
Long chain: 7ds P 7ds.
They are not worked in this particular order, but in different combinations, therefore the instruction RV cannot be included. RV is necessary of course between ring and chain and taken for granted. Build on to the first round by starting a scallop with a ring, joining to the fourth ring from the corner, on the short side. This will leave one free ring and chain at the end of the first round. Then work the short chain. A ring and long chain follow, which pair is worked three times in succession: then ring, short chain and ring, which concludes the scallop. This last ring joins to the ring next to the corner, so that two rings of the first round remain free.
Abbreviated, the scallop would read:
Ring: short chain: 3(ring: long chain) ring.
Short chain: ring (RV occurring after each unit) which is one repetition of the second round. You have now arrived at the corner. The corner scallop is described as the corner circle, as it leaves no disengaged rings between start and finish.

The corner circle: This consists of six rings and five long chains. As given in the formula, it would read: 5(R long Ch) R. The first ring joins to the nearest picot on the corner ring:

the last to its remaining free picot, so completing the corner circle.

A new scallop is now started, worked as the first, its first ring joining to the ring above it (next to the corner), its last to the fourth from the corner. Note that between the scallops and the corner circle, and between adjoining scallops, two rings lie next to one another, but facing away: there is no chain between them. To follow the model, work one more scallop, joining its first ring to the next ring on the first round. On completion there will be one ring of the first round standing free, at the end of the line, to which the next scallop would join. It is shown in the model Fig. I. 14.

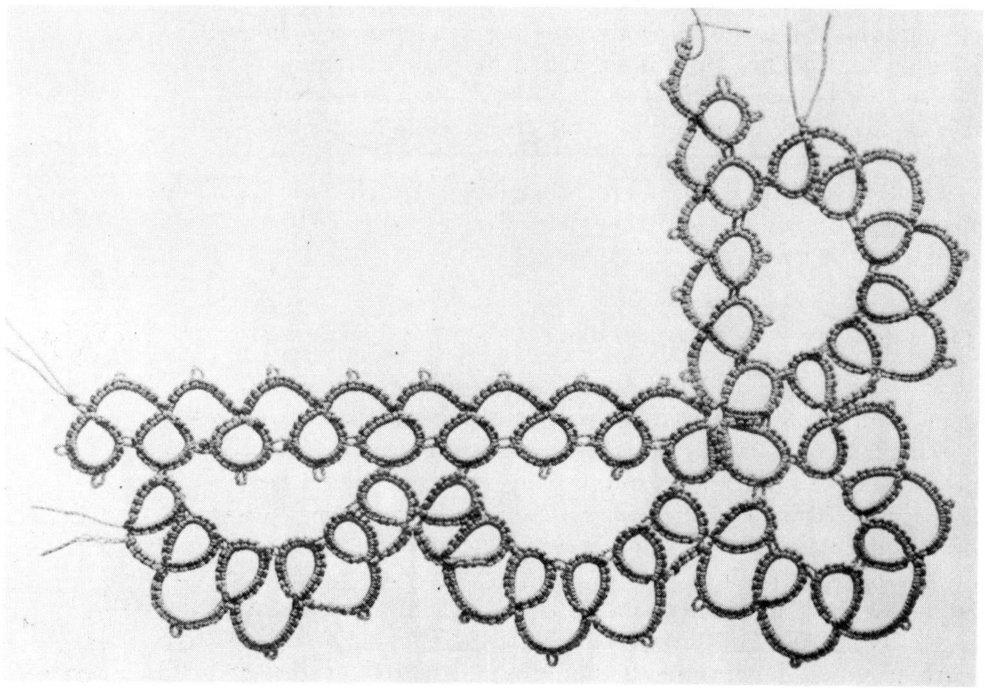

Fig. I 14

Repetition balance

The application of one round to another, when their repetitions do not correspond in length, as in the above example, introduces the subject of repetition balance, an important aspect of design. In this double edging, one scallop engages four rings of the first row, counting those from which it starts and ends, plus the two in between. Therefore the first row must consist of multiples of four repetitions. If more, or less, you will end up with half a scallop. In working round a square, multiples of four must be on each side. At present you need not be concerned with this, but you would be if you wanted to make a square, or a strip of an exact length to fit a piece of fabric. The scallops determine its size.

The examples that follow are shown much enlarged, so that the reader wishing to work them can easily count the stitches.

STRAIGHT LINES INTO CIRCLES

A straight line is the most basic of geometrical forms. We have been concentrating on straight lines, i.e. edgings, even though they were actually built up of rings and chains. A circle is a line whose end is joined to the start (a very loose definition) and it is this, the most interesting of forms, which we now study. This study is simplified if we first examine two small groupings, both of which occur so frequently that it is an advantage to be familiar with them before analysing the circle and its composition.

These two classical forms are so old, and of such widespread use (in edgings too) that they have earned titles for themselves by which they are known.

The Clover

This is a grouping of three rings. A short portion of chain often leads up to it, and follows it, but the actual clover is the three rings only. The rings, which are joined, can be all one size (a trefoil) but usually the centre one is larger, flanked by a smaller one on either side. The overall size, proportions, the position of the joins and any ornamental picots are all variables, selected according to the requirements of the pattern including it. In some patterns, clovers (without chains) are used to hold parts of the main work together, independently made and inserted at the finish. To work it well, the rings must be very close together. When they are worked, fold the piece in half to start the following chain. This will ensure that the bases are as near together as possible. Two clovers are shown in Fig. I. 15.

Fig. I 15

The Scroll

This is a ring followed by a chain, the two alternating and forming one repetition if their respective sizes remain constant. It is much used, many patterns consisting of it exclusively. It can form a 'line' or be brought round to meet itself, rings facing out, chains in. Three repetitions would make a triangle, four a square and five a pentagon. Six will form a circle, shown in Fig. I. 16. Admittedly this title of scroll, which is mine, is not in common use, but I hope it will become so. By identifying a formation which is repeated and giving it a name, the description of patterns can be simplified and thereby shortened.

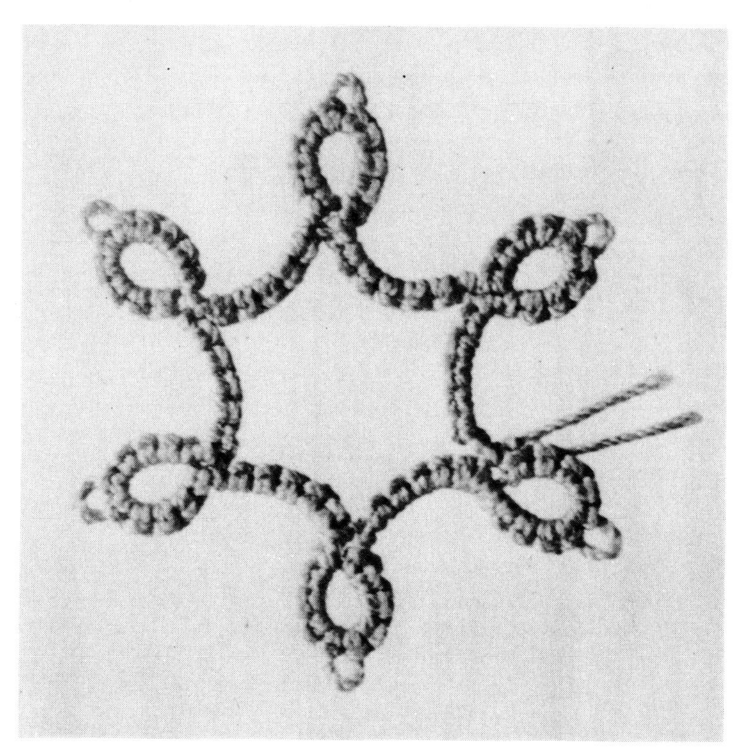

Fig. I 16

THE MEDALLION

This is a circular piece, whose pictorial effect or design is obtained by dividing it into a given number of equal parts. The design therefore dictates the number of repetitions required to form it. Theoretically there can be any number, but the usual working range lies between three and twelve. Six, eight and twelve are the most common: four is more used for squares. The uneven numbers, three, five and seven, are more difficult to design, and do not appear so often, but they are just as workable and effective.

Classification of medallions

Medallions can be classified from two independent points of view. The first refers to the number of repetitions which compose it. The second is based on the physical construction of the actual centre-piece, whose parts—even if only a space—are shared by each repetition. There are only three types, and every medallion is built round one of them, distinguishing it from the other two. What happens afterwards in ensuing rounds is so various that the physical classification ends there. Any number of repetitions can be associated with any type of centre: the two are independent.

The three centres:

(1) The enclosed space
(2) The centre picot
(3) The central ring.

These three were probably evolved in this order. Tatting began with a row of unjoined rings, drawn round to form an enclosure, circular or oval. The latter was known as a 'lozenge', often filled in with needlework. The rings could face in or out. Much later, with the arrival of chains, both together formed the enclosure, and sometimes chains alone. All occur in present-day patterns, for the enclosed space, large or small, allows more originality in design.

1. The enclosed space:

Examples, scroll and trefoil.

The Scroll, Fig. I. 17: In the description of the formation of a scroll (shown in the previous figure) the illustration showed one of six repetitions drawn into a circle, which automatically encloses a space: it is a free-standing example of this type of centre, composed of both ring and chain. It can equally well be drawn round in the opposite direction, rings facing in: in this case the rings alone form the space. The chains are beyond it, cut off by the joins of the rings. Six rings of this size are not quite enough: eight are used. Additional rounds can be built on these two figures to produce medallions, with rather large interior spaces.

As a contrast, an extremely neat one is shown, in a completed medallion from an Australian pattern described as the Trefoil.

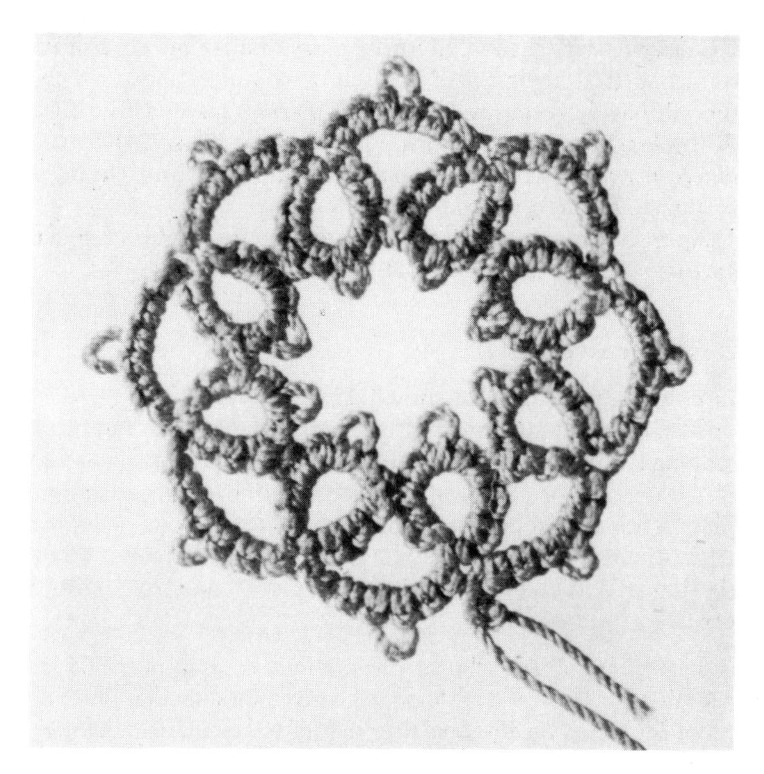

Fig. I 17

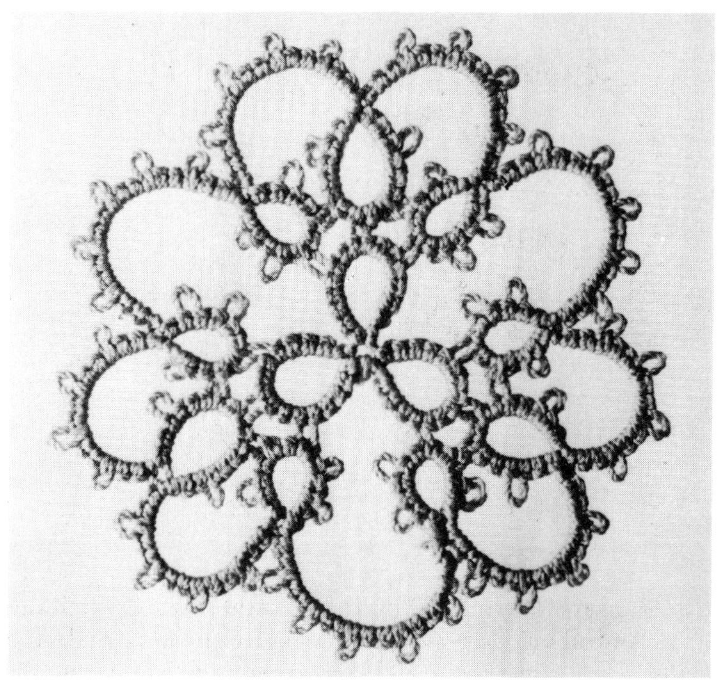

Fig. I 18

The Trefoil, Fig. I. 18: The three rings of a trefoil are drawn round so that their bases encircle a minute space, which, though barely recognisable, counts as one, formed by rings. A broken scroll surrounds the trefoil—broken because between every two repetitions of a small ring and chain, a larger couple intervenes.

Apart from this particular example, the enclosed space and its components are usually easy to identify.

2. The centre picot:

Examples, a square and snowflake.

This is an old form related to the enclosed space, and often looking rather like it, but lying at the centre is a picot carried on either ring or chain, into which ensuing work joins. The picot is not apparent as such: it should be completely covered with stitches, and made just large enough to accommodate the joins. You can only achieve its correct size by trial and error.

A square, Fig. I. 19: Shows the nucleus of a square of four repetitions. It is a simple scroll with rings facing in. The picot is carried on the first ring made, to which others join.

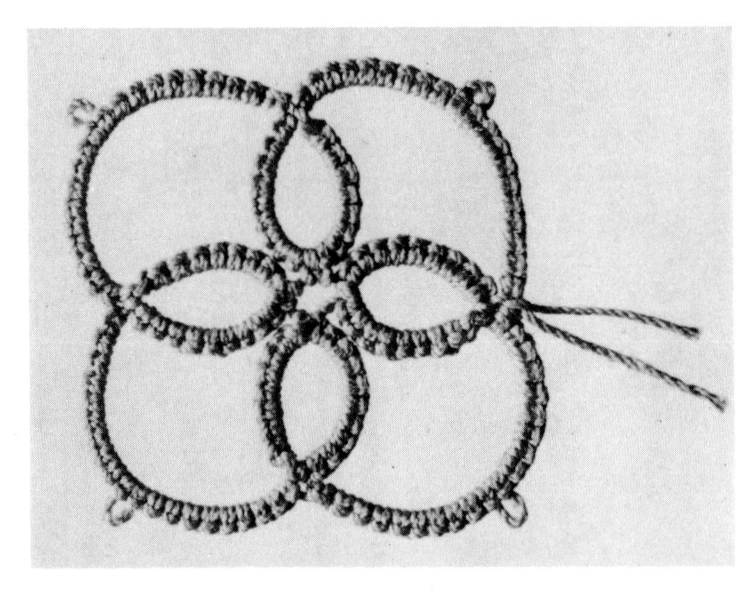

Fig. I 19

The Snowflake, Fig. I. 20: This is a medallion of six repetitions (also Australian) demonstrating a centre picot carried on a chain. The chains, two to a spoke, are worked to and from the centre, each joining into the picot as it reaches it. The edge of the piece is composed of six clovers, each worked between two single chains, thus the first and last chain meet to form one complete spoke. The piece, which starts with a clover, is worked on one pair of threads.

This type of centre, at one time neglected, now occurs frequently in modern patterns. The picot can be at the *start* of a chain, an unusual construction and more difficult to identify.

Fig. I 20

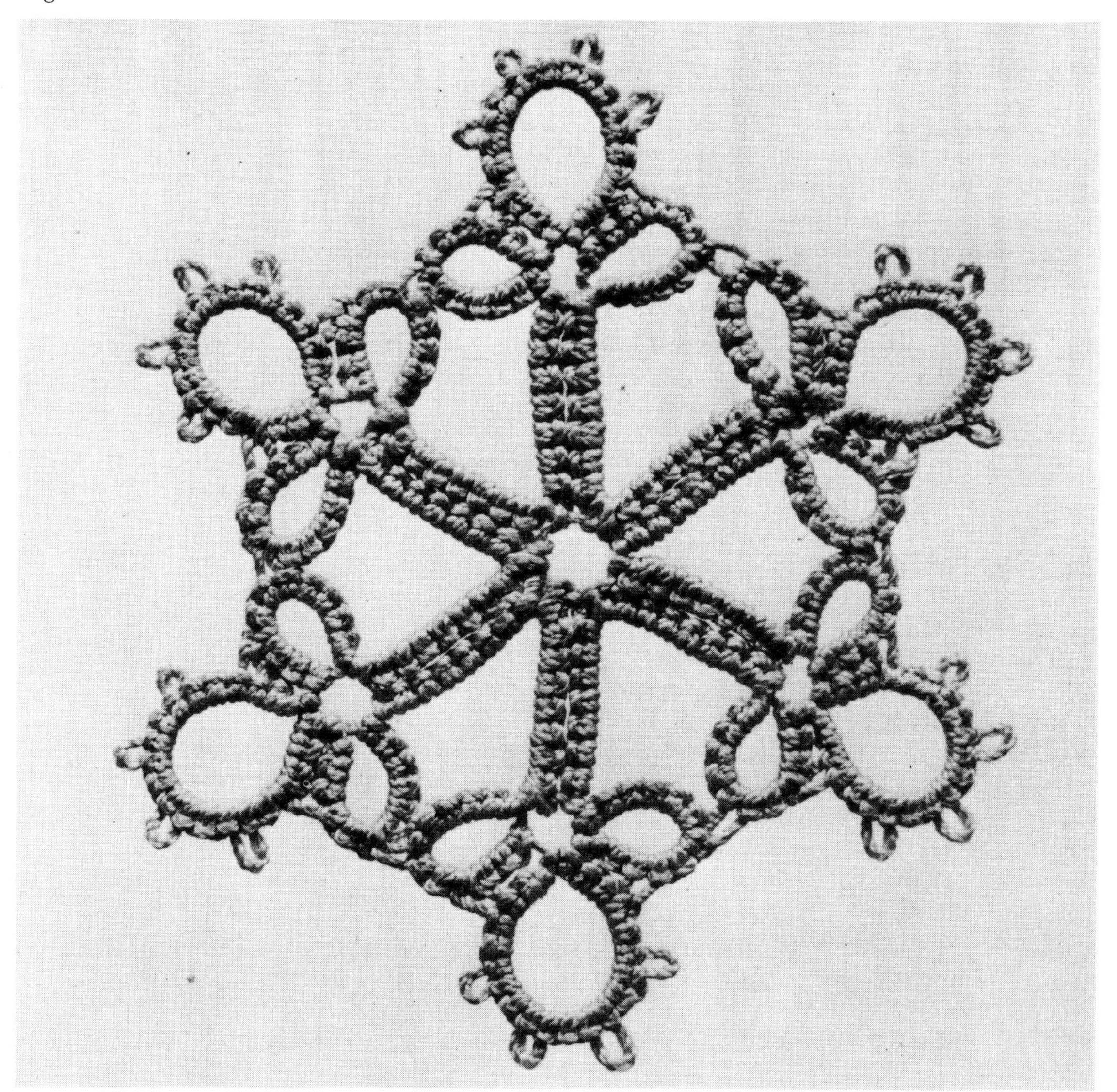

3. The central ring:

The Daisy, Wheel and a Star.

Now in very common use, the central ring probably succeeded the centre picot; its identification is easy. A ring carrying equally spaced picots is worked, the thread (usually) cut off on conclusion. A round on a new thread joins to the picots on the ring, which is the centre of the piece. Of the three examples given, two are all ring, the third includes a chain.

The Daisy, Fig. I. 21: This piece, of six repetitions, is rather primitive, the whole being worked on the one shuttle thread. It is shown because in this particular case, the thread forming the central ring is not cut off but retained to work the encircling round of rings or petals. This involves joins with the running thread to the picots on the central ring, which requires practice to do neatly. It is quick to work, being all on the one thread, and forms a good solid centre, provided the picots are small and the joins very close in. The petals are identical, joining to one another; they carry five ornamental picots.

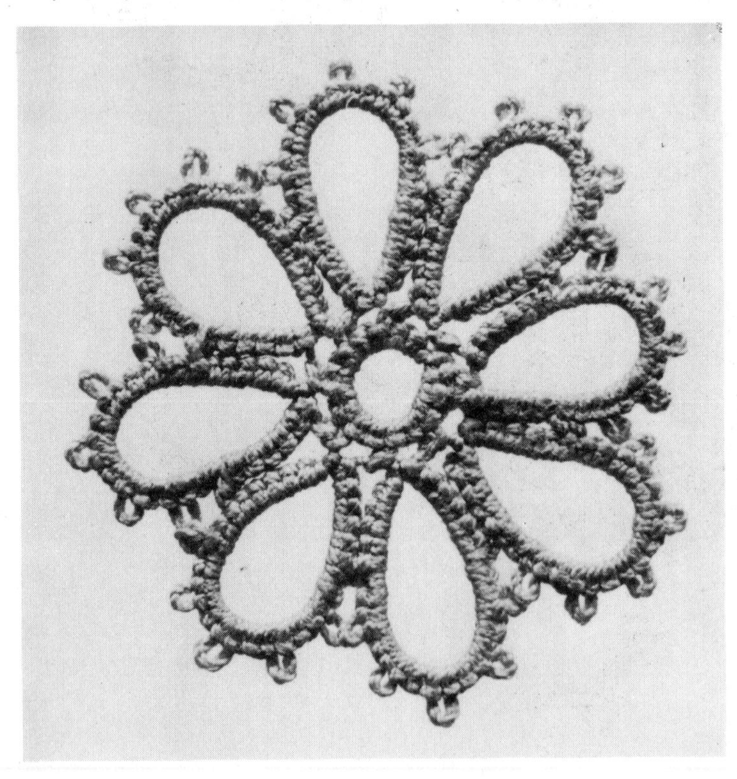

Fig. I 21

The Wheel, Fig. I. 22: This is another and long-established classical formation, known by name. Surrounding the central ring, which carries at least eight picots, but usually twelve or more, two doubles apart, the following round starts with a small ring, joining into one of the central picots halfway through its construction. The ring is completed, the work reversed, and a larger ring is worked a short distance away, leaving a space of thread between them. These two rings form the repetition of the round. The work is reversed after

Fig. I 22

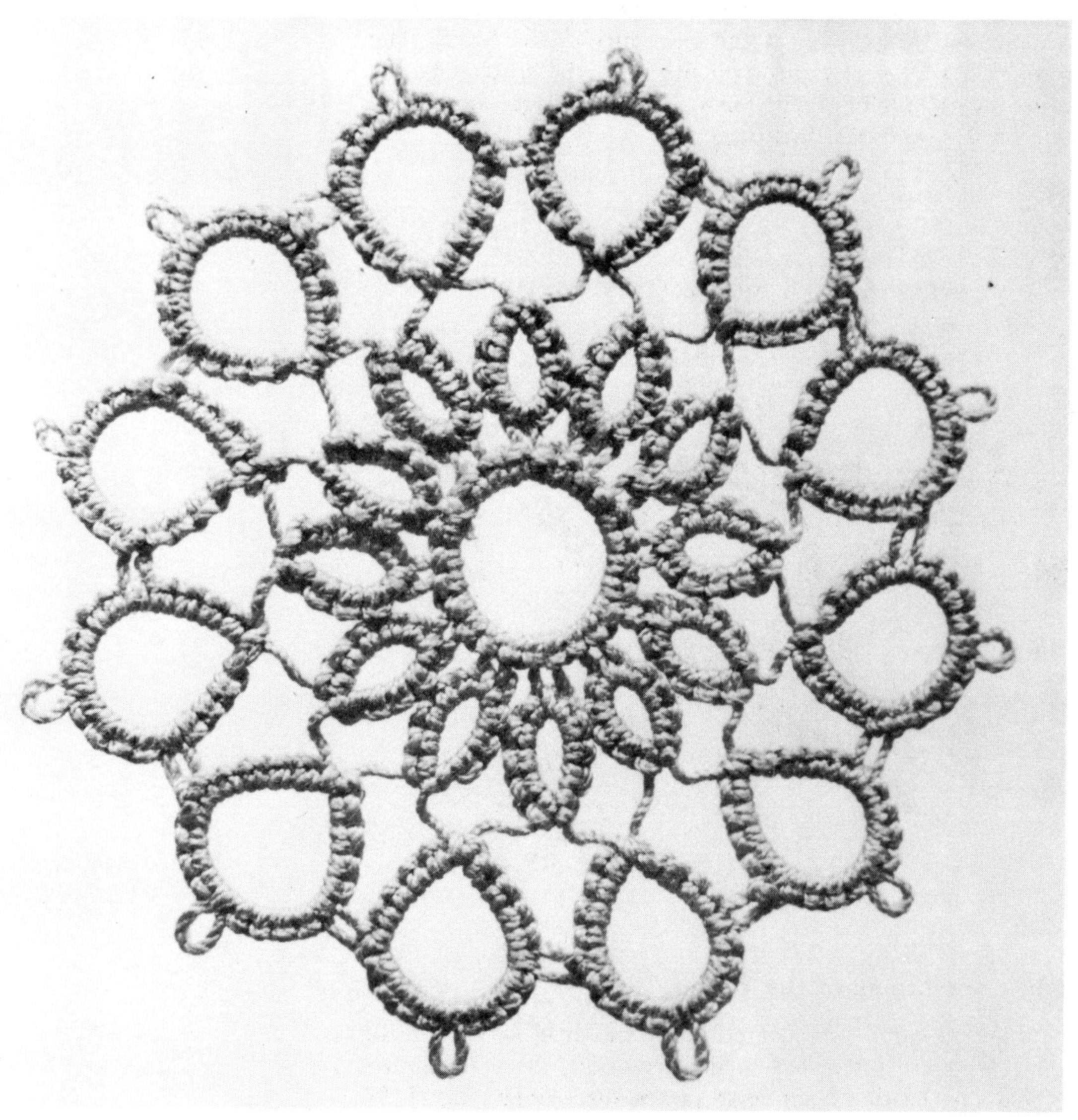

every ring (their bases are opposite to one another) and the thread tied finally into the start of the round—the first small ring. This is the basic wheel, but they often carry an additional round, attached to the larger outer rings, which are usually joined on either side.

A Star, Fig. I. 23: The Star, of five repetitions, is simple but not a beginner's piece; it is not easy to work well. The central ring, which is comparatively large, carries five picots, equally spaced. It is surrounded by a scroll on a new pair of threads, the chains joining to the picots, the small ornamented rings lying at the extremity of the 'rays'. The scroll starts from any picot on the ring, the stitches facing into the triangles they form. Rather slack but even tension is essential in this piece.

Fig. I 23

Some variations of the Wheel:

The Wheel can be elaborated in a number of ways, and for those who are interested in its formation, three examples, which are hardly beginners' pieces, are given. Fig. I. 24

shows the central ring carrying twelve picots which are crossed when picked up by the ensuing round. Fig. I. 25 carries twelve very long picots, picked up by large and highly ornamented rings. The outer row consists of pairs of plain rings instead of one alone, which would be disproportionately large. Fig. I. 26 is worked in fine thread. The central ring carries eight small picots. The small rings joining to them are separated by comparatively long spaces of thread. On completion of this round the ends are cut off. The following round—in and out in the correct manner—consists of small rings in and small rings out, which last carry three fairly long picots. Two of the small inner rings link into each space of thread, instead of to a picot, therefore there are a total of sixteen facing each way. The outer round consists of sixteen rings, unjoined, and worked independently, then sewn on with a needle in the Victorian style. This model is not a true wheel, owing to the additional round joining to the centre, but it can be described as built up on wheel formation.

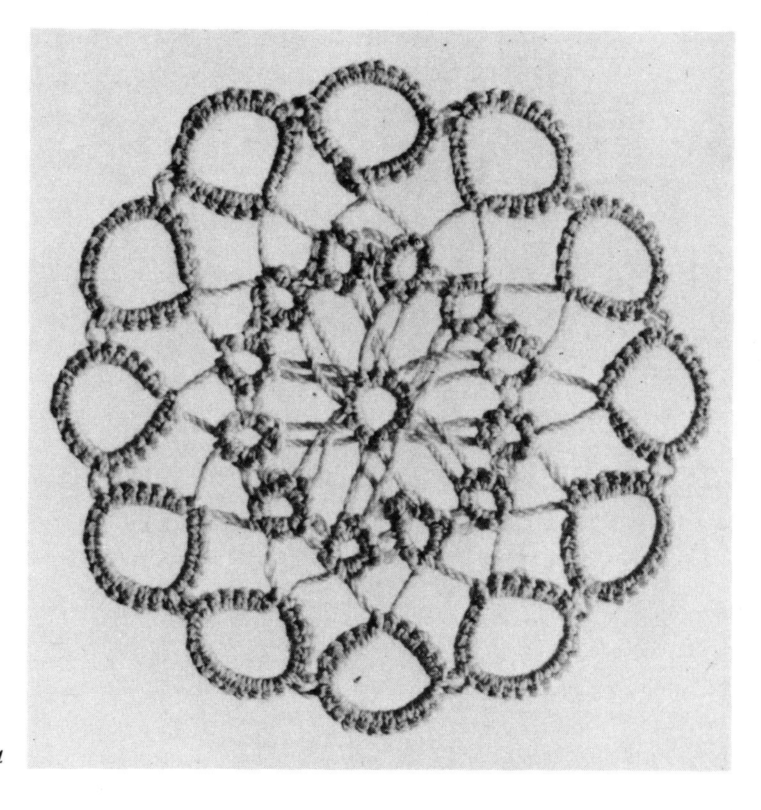

Fig. I 24

Fig. I 25

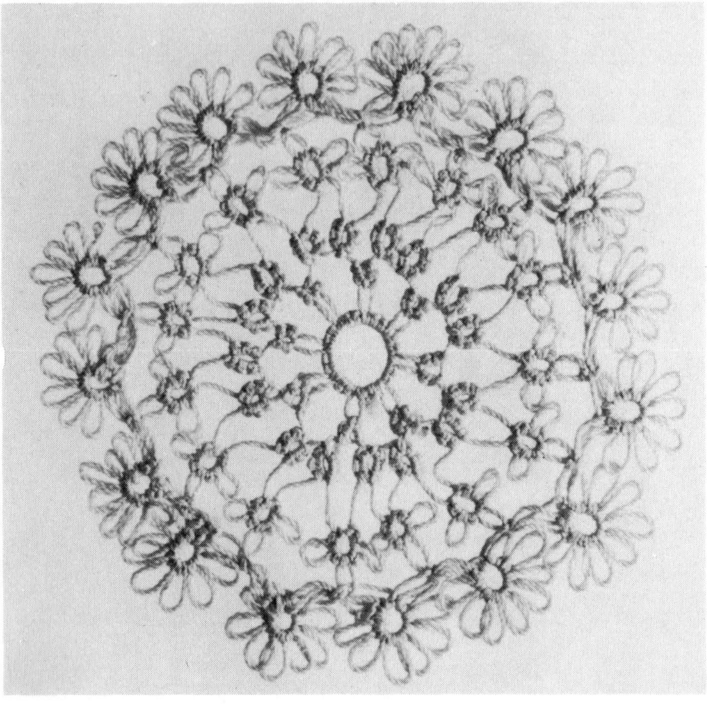

Fig. I 26

DESCRIBING A MEDALLION

Look at and examine all the patterns of medallions that you have, and identify the type of centre, and what composes it. (Look also for clovers and scrolls, in edgings as well). This advance knowledge is of great help towards understanding a complicated piece, whatever the style of writing the pattern may be. Your pattern book is not likely to give a description: write one yourself before you begin to work. Do not be confused by excessive ornament: it has nothing to do with structure. The description of a medallion should start with a brief account of its characteristics. The number of repetitions and its centre are the most important. This should be followed by the number of rounds, the position of the starting point if obscure, and any other special feature it may show. Such an analysis before beginning to work, will save you time and uncertainty. Methods of construction are infinite: they are the most interesting of all shapes.

THREAD ENDS

Finishing off

To conceal the ends at the conclusion of work, sew them for a short distance to the underside of the last piece(s) made, with matching cotton: then cut off. Alternatively, stick them down with an adhesive, and cut. This can be invisible on the upper surface.

Joining a new thread

A join means the presence of two ends, that of the old thread and the start of the new, and to get rid of either, the pattern must consist of ring and chain alternately. Both the auxiliary and the shuttle thread can be replaced, one at a time, each requiring one ring and one chain for the operation. The join must take place *after* a chain in both cases. The principle is to integrate one of the ends into the ensuing ring, and the other into the ensuing chain, while under construction, where for three doubles it runs alongside the running thread. Alternatively it could accompany the thread making the stitches (in a chain only) which method is easier to work, but it makes the chain rather thick, to be avoided if possible. When the end is secure, it is abandoned, and the work continues normally. The end is now sticking out of the work on one side, and is eventually cut off short. For convenience in handling, both thread ends, the old and the new, should be about six inches long and threaded on needles.

To replace the auxiliary thread

Start the ring with one stitch (single), turned, but very loose and open. Pass the end of the new thread (on a needle) through the stitch, following the passage of the running thread. Push the stitch back as close to the preceding chain as possible, pulling the *stitch* thread very tightly. Then make the second half, passing the needle through it, as before. Continue in this manner for three doubles, which are now carried on two running threads. Now abandon the new end and continue the ring. Draw it up: tighten also the thread on the needle. It does not matter if it slips: it will tighten as soon as it is worked into the chain. Before you draw up, make sure that the new auxiliary is not caught above the ring: it must lie beneath it. At the base of the ring there will be three threads, the shuttle, the new auxiliary and the end of the old one, on a needle. Work the chain, very close in, integrating this last into the first three doubles as before, then abandoning it and continuing normally. When finished, cut off the ends closely. Shown in the diagram Fig. I. 27a.

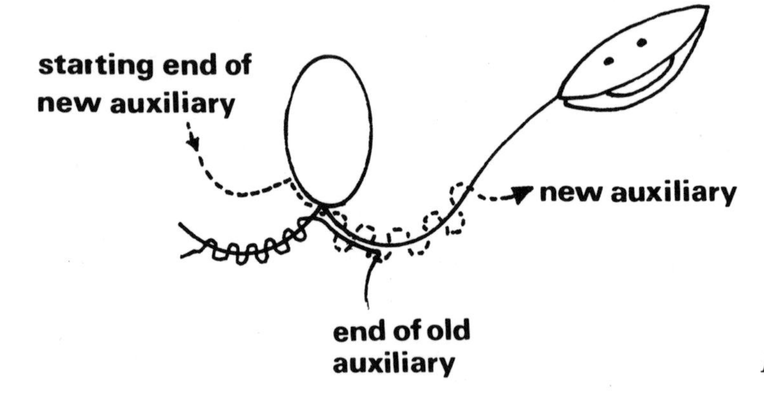

Fig. I 27a

To replace the shuttle thread

This is rather more difficult. Cut off the old shuttle, leaving the 6 inches, threaded on a needle. Start a ring on a new shuttle with one half-stitch, very loose as before, bring it up to the work and pass the old shuttle end through it, following the course of the running thread. Keep the ring about an

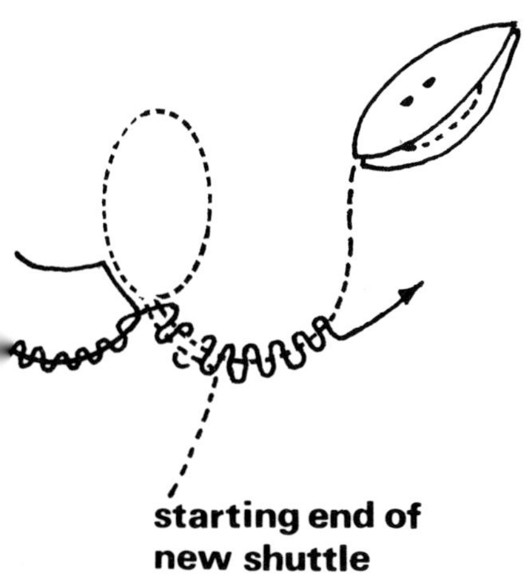

Fig. I 28a

inch away from the preceding chain. Tighten the stitch and continue for a total of three doubles, concealing the old thread. Then abandon the end and continue normally. Draw up the ring, and then pull the old shuttle end very tightly—this will bring the ring close up to the previous chain. At the base there will be three threads: the new shuttle: the auxiliary, and the starting end of new shuttle thread also on a needle. Start the chain, incorporating this last for the first three doubles, as before. Abandon it, and finish the chain. Shown in the diagram Fig. I. 28a.

To replace both threads simultaneously is actually easier, as on a continuous thread you have no starts to conceal. Work a new ring, absorbing the old shuttle end, and in the following chain, conceal the old auxiliary.

UNDOING THE WORK

You can undo a chain fairly easily by loosening the stitches with a pin, and passing the shuttle thread back through them, one at a time. A ring is much more difficult, if drawn up it is generally considered as a lost cause! If its tension is not too tight, you may be able to loosen the last two stitches to make a loop large enough to pass the shuttle through. You are actually capsizing each stitch, transferring it back to the running thread. Then loosen two more. There must always be two loose at a time to give a long enough loop to make the transfer. It is a waste of time undoing too much. It is better to cut back the work to the offending part, undoing just enough to give you ends to work with—say an inch—and tie on new threads, but you should of course use the concealment method if you can. The ends, which will be short, can be drawn through the stitches with the hook instead of a needle: some workers prefer the hook in any case.

FINISHING

Washing, stiffening, stretching, pressing.

Workers who have clean dry hands at all times will not need to wash their piece when completed. Some of us, however, do not have this advantage, and it will have to be either washed or dry-cleaned. To dry-clean, lay the work out flat on paper, dust thickly with French chalk, and leave overnight. Then shake out the chalk. If the piece is mounted, go over it with a very soft brush.

Washing is necessary for articles that have been exposed and used for some time. The correct way to wash lace is to tack it flat on a piece of white flannel, lay in a flat dish and cover with warm soap-suds. Or sew the flannel round a bottle and plunge up and down in a deep saucepan: it can simmer for a little while. Rinse and leave to dry.

Real lace as a rule is neither stiffened nor pressed, but if you want to stiffen work which is too slack to hold its shape, use a solution of borax, or sugar, in the last rinsing water; removing it from the flannel. When nearly dry place the piece upside down on several layers of soft material and press lightly. Pressing tatting is rather hazardous owing to the presence of ornamental picots, which should stand out clearly: pressing tends to crush them out of shape. It is really better to stretch the piece on a board, a pin in every picot if necessary: wet thoroughly and leave to dry. An exhibition piece, washed or not, should always be stretched thus, using of course rustless pins. This not only ensures that the picots are in position, but that the piece holds its correct shape. Washing and quick drying will give it a certain stiffness without extra help. The pins must be very firmly inserted in a soft-wood board. Use a thimble to press them in.

WHAT TO DO WITH TATTING

There are three ways of using the work. It can be a complete object of practical use, a trimming to some other article, and a decorative ornament in itself. In the first group it appears as mats of all kinds and sizes, a collar, a pair of gloves, a baby's fitted bonnet, etc. Two medallions, lined and hinged together, make an attractive cover for a powder-compact. A modern Swedish book, *Frivoliteter*, by Elwy Persson and Gun Blomqvist, gives complete bridal crowns, stiffened. On a large scale it can make an entire dress, appropriately lined. It falls well and gracefully.

As a trimming: if by trimming we mean a non-essential added to an existing article, thereby improving its appearance, the opportunities have never been so great as they are today. In wearing apparel it is acceptable as decoration on many articles, being adaptable to any type of dress, a formal wedding outfit, or the practical apron. In dress it can make the yoke of a blouse (mounted on net if very fine): big starched turn-back cuffs. Edgings to collars, underwear, and especially to handkerchiefs and table-mats are familiar to all.

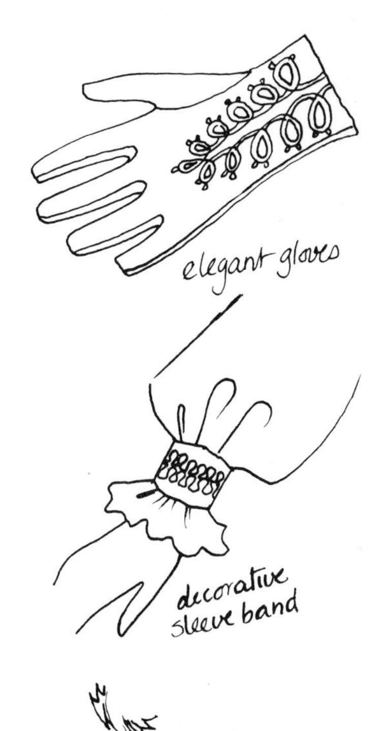

For dress accessories: a simple chain makes excellent 'loop' buttonholes (described in Part II) and slots for belts. Buttons themselves can be produced by sewing a very small medallion to a circle of fabric to be secured to a button mould. An edging or narrow insertion can be sewn on a velvet ribbon for a choker collar. Tatting can decorate an evening bag, spectacle-case, and fan. If in fine thread or silk, it will not interfere with the folding of the fan. A medallion can be pinned, with a suitable brooch in the centre, to the lapel of a jacket.

For millinery it can make ornaments for hats, a bride's headdress and veil.

For household articles: on lampshades, cover for the Radio Times, as door plates. For these the tatting is mounted on stiffened fabric and set behind glass (standard size 11″ × 3″).

Miscellaneous articles include trimmings on dress for puppets, dolls, and furnishings for dolls' houses: book markers.

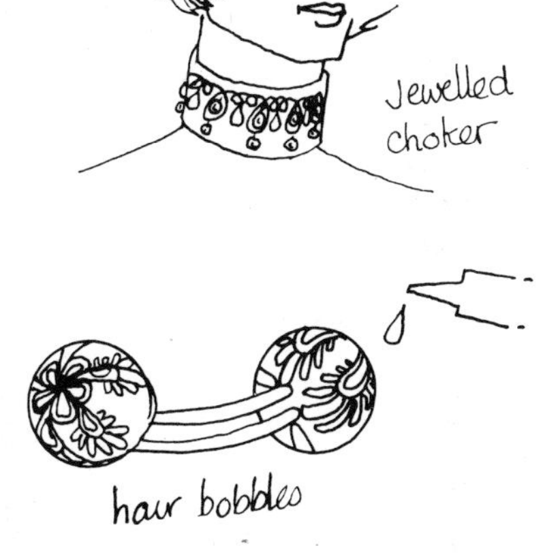

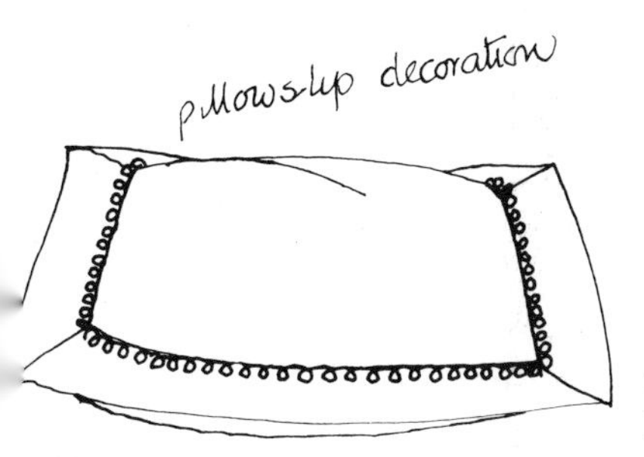

Church work

This is a specialised field, concerned with decoration to both vestments and church furnishings. For vestments, ornament (in traditional designs) on stoles: deep lace borders to surplices, plaques for copes, especially in the Greek Church. This work can involve metallic threads and jewels. For furnishings: borders to altar frontals, Bible markers for the lectern, pulpit fall, chalice covers.

Christmas cards

If you make your own cards, a small star, or any other shape, can be glued or sewn on them. Alternatively make one good piece and have it photographed, either to attach to a blank card made of suitable art paper, or printed on the card itself.

Tatting as pure decoration

Many mats, and medallions, which are the nucleus of mats, are sufficiently attractive to display as decoration on their own. A Swedish arrangement is to suspend them as a string of mobiles, in which case they are suitably stiffened. Alternatively they may be mounted on fabric and framed as a picture. One of the advantages of mounting is the absence of thread ends. They are drawn through to the back of the fabric and secured with Sellotape. To mount successfully is not easy. It involves the selection of the background, whose colour and texture has a great influence on the appearance of the work. The style and size of the frame is equally important, and it should be fitted with a fillet to keep the glass—preferably Perspex—from touching the surface.

CONCLUSION

If you have absorbed the technique so far described, you now have a solid groundwork of good tatting practice. You are now ready to experiment with the special arrangements demonstrated in Part II.

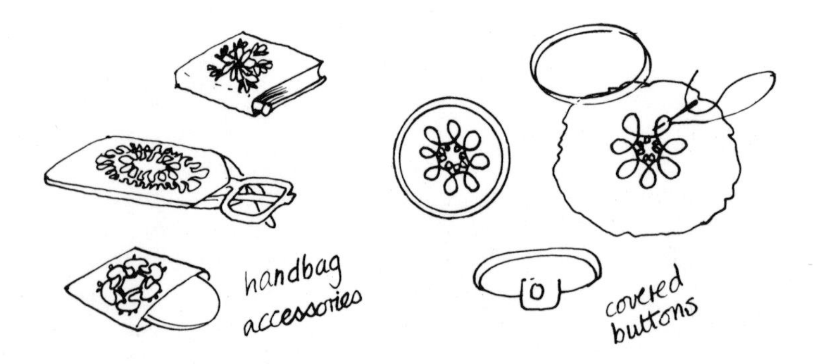

Part II

ENLARGING THE SCOPE

FOREWORD

During the evolution of tatting, two of its pioneers, Elénore Riego de la Branchardière, and an Englishwoman, Lady Hoare, had considerable influence on the work. Riego, as she was always known, half Irish, and half French, published twelve little pattern books, the first dated 1850. At that time neither the chain nor the join had been invented, but she produced a number of new arrangements which she called 'my improvements'. Many of these are now obsolete, but some are worth revival, and several of the modern designs in this book are developed from them, inspired by her.

More than 50 years later, in 1910, Lady Hoare, with an established technique on which to build, published *The Art of Tatting*, usually known as 'Lady Hoare's Book'. In this she collaborated with Queen Marie of Roumania, an indefatigable tatter, who produced in great quantity vestments and furnishings for the Greek Orthodox Church. Between them they carried the work a great deal further in both design and construction.

Tatting owes much to these dedicated women, but the creations of the pioneer are valueless unless absorbed into general practice. Your contribution to this honourable but modest craft can both keep it alive and increase its scope still further, for there is still much more that could be done. Every aspect of the work can be involved to some degree, and suggestions for obtaining variations from classical styles are here presented, for the extraordinary versatility of the stitch has not yet been fully exploited. Some are no doubt familiar to many workers, although they are not in current pattern books. The continuous thread, anticipated by Riego, is one of these, but although usually neglected by English pattern writers, I consider it important enough to be learned at the start, and not treated as 'special'.

The procedures are arranged in a logical order, starting with the raw material and the instrument—the Thread and the Shuttle. The Stitch, Tension, the Ring, Chain, Picot and Join, are then examined, showing what they have done, and what they may yet do. In this order, one of the more elaborate techniques appears at the beginning, and some of the easiest and most useful at the end, but it is the most practical way of presenting them. Overmuch attention need not be given to Pearl Tatting, described under the Thread, or to the use of a second shuttle. The third section, on the Stitch, is the most important in the list, and it is suggested that you first concentrate on this.

THE THREAD

Lady Hoare writes: '[Linen] Thread evenly spun is far better for use than cotton, and this can now be easily procured in many colours. The DMC's catalogue gives a long list of flax spun in varying degrees of fineness and colour which tat well and easily. Silk is also an excellent material to use and the same company sell the most beautiful silks in good colours. It is also easier to tat in silk than in thread. H.M. the Queen of Roumania has made many beautiful designs, using two shades of white silks—a blue and a cream white. This she further enriches with gold thread and jewels. . . .'

This list is an indication of the quality of work and materials at that time. Materials available to us are not so varied. Linen thread (used in lace-making) is hard to find evenly spun. Sewing silk is possible but it is too fine for ordinary work. The Queen's silk was obviously thicker. Sewing silk shows to best advantage in long picots, i.e. as an unworked thread—the sheen is lost in tight rings and chains. As for gold and silver: most metallic threads are now flat, for machine work: for tatting they must be circular.

Regarding cotton: DMC do still supply it in a number of good colours, especially made for tatting, in No. 70 only. If you can work with one so fine, you will notice the difference between it and the crochet cotton available to us, which for firm tatting is rather too loose and soft: made for crochet in fact. Terylene (Dacron) is sometimes preferred by fine workers. Cotton does, however, have much to recommend it. It is cheaper than other threads, has a pleasant bloom, is strong and washable, and can produce some fine pieces of work.

Different calibres of the same thread used together

A thick cotton may be on the shuttle, working over a thinner ball. The result is a slender, very compact chain. Conversely a thin shuttle thread may support a thick ball, giving a somewhat thicker chain with larger stitches: it will also be longer, if the same number is worked in both sections. It is useful when representing an object, where strokes of two thicknesses are an advantage.

Mixed threads of different materials

The gold and silver threads used by Queen Marie constituted

the auxiliary, thick white silk forming the running line. With the many new threads now appearing, though not intended for tatting, new mixtures should be possible. They do not have to possess all the necessary properties, provided they are associated with one that does.

Additional threads in shuttle and/or ball

Two or more threads wound together on a shuttle will produce a thicker ring—both running thread and stitches are involved. In chains the extra one can accompany shuttle, ball, or both together. Double threads will disorganise the natural curve of the chain, which will be straight. On a mount it can be arranged to stand on its stitches, so that they lie underneath, and the upper surface is smooth, an advantage in working stalks and stems. A strand of sewing silk of appropriate colour can be wound on either or both shuttles with the cotton, treating the two as one. This gives interest to flower petals. Double silk threads are practicable: they give body to one another.

Tatting therefore need not always be composed of a single thread of cotton, as is generally supposed. For special effects, particularly in flower work, the addition of other threads gives a much more realistic effect. An old style, Pearl tatting, made use of multiple ball threads, but worked individually into the chain, thus alternating two balls. It had apparently a short life, but it was such a new step in tatting practice that a description of it is worth recording.

Pearl tatting

This was offered by Riego, originally under the title of Pearl Beading. There were two forms, single and double. Single Pearl employs one extra thread.

The extra thread is used as an auxiliary, worked alternately with the normal one but on the opposite side of the running thread, so that its stitches face down. It is almost essential to be able to work the stitch upside down—for which directions are given in the next section—otherwise it will be necessary to reverse the work after every double. To make it easier to see what you are doing, use another colour for this thread, as in the model.

Assume that you are using black and white. On a continuous black thread (shuttle and ball) start with one double in the normal way, for a blind end. Then take the white thread, leaving a few inches of 'tail', and work one double with it, to face down towards you, tight up against the black stitch. Repeat these two doubles, black up, white down, keeping the auxiliaries as tight as possible. The result is a stiff flat straight chain, with no natural curve, slightly wider than the normal and carrying very small pearls (not true picots for which you leave a space) on both sides. Variation is produced by increasing the number of doubles to two or more, with each ball thread, which will make larger pearls: if you leave a space intentionally then they will be larger still.

The model (Fig. II. 1) shows a chain with three variations. The first group has minimum size pearls on both sides. The second carries two consecutive doubles on each thread, and also leaves a space. At first longer pearls are made on the black thread only: the whites are kept as tight as possible, as at the start. After six long black there are six long white; then a section with long on both sides.

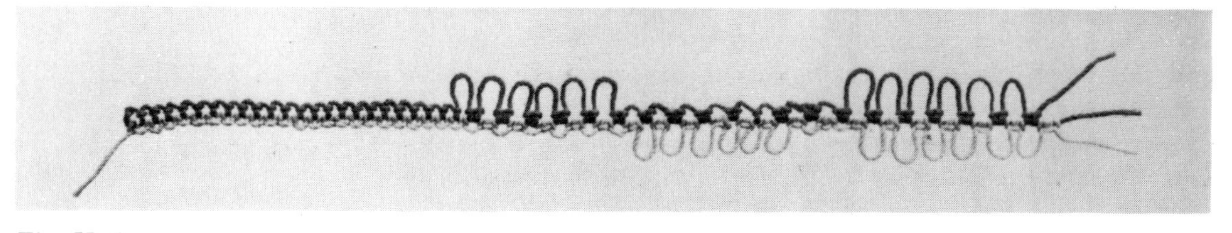

Fig. II 1

The Pearl chain may be straight, (slightly) convex, or concave, all three forms depending on the sequence of the stitches, explained in the Stitch section. For a straight chain, work 1 plain, one purl (abbreviated to 1 pl 1 pu) (for each double-stitch) on the upper edge, 1 pu 1 pl on the lower. For a convex curve, 1 pl 1 pu on *both edges.* This is used for small circles. For concave, 1 pu 1 pl on both, reversing the order of the convex. Sections of the two curves may be alternated to give an undu.ating line. Two such lines, crossing one another at the change of sequence, make an attractive cable.

'Double pearl' uses an extra *pair* of threads, added to the single. There are therefore two auxiliaries on either side, each worked alternately. A detailed description of the model is not given, but Fig. II. 2 shows a fairly simple example, and also the threads in position for the start.

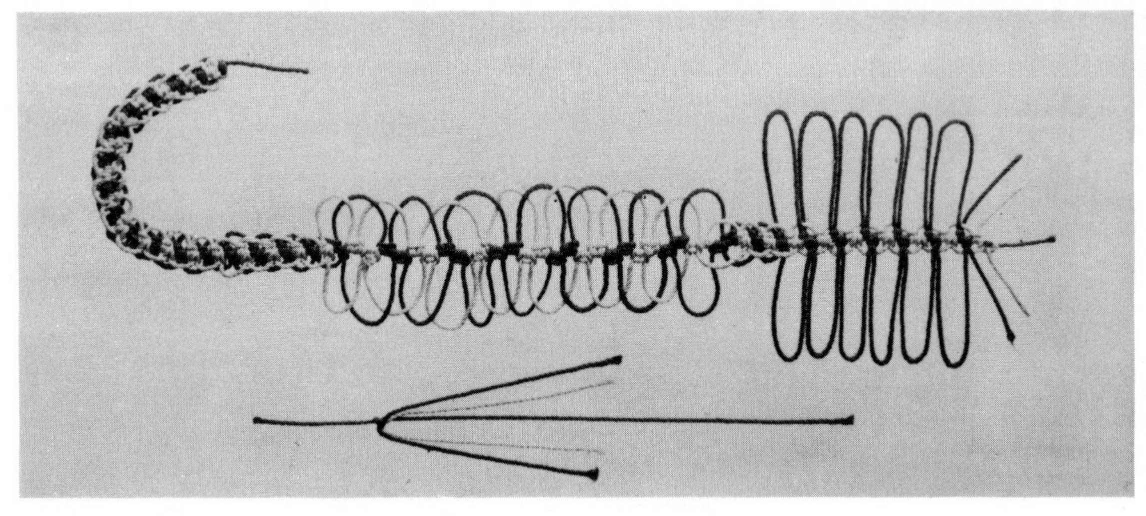

Fig. II 2

Application of pearl tatting

I have not been able to find, in any old books, suggestions for its use, but in imaginative hands it could surely produce something acceptable to the time. Once you have established the rhythm of the repetition it is fun to do, for it gives quick and bold results. Because of its rigidity it can produce strong independent pieces, which could be used for trimming on dress or millinery. Apart from pure ornament it has its use in combination with other work, for with pearls on both edges it can make joins on both sides. An example is shown in a medallion, where the upper thread of a pearl chain is on a second shuttle to perform work of its own, and the lower joins to an interior centre piece, described in the section on the Picot (p. 79).

THE SHUTTLE

A second working shuttle is known to many workers, but often avoided by the beginner as it sounds more complicated. Actually it is not. The work is usually simplified, and greater flexibility in design becomes possible.

Normally the auxiliary thread is passive, employed by the shuttle thread. If it is wound on a second shuttle, it too can become active, i.e. it can make rings on its own. With it, a ring can be carried on or 'thrown off' from a chain at any point, without disturbing the running thread whose tension remains unbroken. When the ring is closed, the thread which made it returns to the chain as the auxiliary. It must be pulled in tightly so that the ring fits squarely down on the chain, which should show no interruption. If you need to make a ring, the chains on either side of it facing *up*, as referred to in the paragraph Reversing the Work (p. 21), the second shuttle will allow you to do this without crossing the threads, and without reversing between units. This is the simplest example of the use of two working shuttles; the chapter on the Chain will describe a few more.

THE STITCH

The three following paragraphs might have been included in the description of the Knot, in Part I, but since the work can be performed without this information, it has not been given until now. A closer understanding of the stitch and its construction is now essential if you intend to follow more advanced patterns.

Renaming its components

The double stitch is a unit composed of a 'first half' and a 'second half', and English patterns refer to them as such. In old books they are named respectively 'plain and purl' stitches. I prefer these words, for they are shorter and more descriptive, implying that the two halves are of different construction. In succeeding descriptions of work, therefore, these terms will be used.

The two surfaces of the work

Make a ring carrying about fifteen adjoining picots all the way round: turn it over and note the difference. On the right side the double stitches show as such, on the internal line of the ring, and the picots have a clear point of emergence from little projections. On the reverse side they do not, and the line is smooth and less interesting. If the stitches are two doubles apart or more, the projections will be visible, but less prominently, lying between picots.

These two effects are produced because the reverse side of a plain stitch appears as a purl, and vice versa. Working right side up, the picot occurs between a purl and a plain. Viewed from the back, it lies between a plain and a purl. The upper side is considered to be more attractive, and is generally presented in the ring. The smooth internal line produced by picots near together, emphasises still more the difference between back and front. Unless you are aware of these two surfaces, it is very easy, when starting a new round on a medallion, to get the centre ring, or groups of rings, wrong side up.

Working the stitch upside down

This is not a stunt, but was quite possibly the method used for the early chain, as no directions appear for reversing between it and a ring. It is a great advantage to be able to do this, for example in a scroll, for by working upside down the stitches are facing in the correct direction without reversing—the same side up is always uppermost.

To practise the motion, start a chain in the normal way for a few stitches. Now reverse the work. You want to continue the chain with the stitches facing the same way, but it is upside down; the shuttle thread is lying above the auxiliary instead of below it, i.e. it is on the far side. Bring the shuttle over towards you, so that it lies across the second thread. To a knitter this would be described as 'wool forward'. Make the stitch normally, but as you slip it back into position hold the shuttle on the far side, so that the stitch will face down in the same position as the others. Continue for a short section, always with 'wool forward' before making a stitch. Reverse and work a few more in the normal way. The object of this piece is simply to prove that whichever way up you work it, the chain remains the same. There will be no indication that parts of it were worked upside down.

The reason why this is so is given below, although it is not necessary to grasp it in order to work it, which you should be able to do from the instructions.

The reason why

If you examine a normally worked chain, worked on the reverse side, although you started with a plain stitch, when viewed from the front this stitch is now a purl. In the upside down chain, although you also started with a plain, this too has become a purl, but this time because you brought the thread forward, which gives the opposite to what you actually worked. The normal chain presents its underside to the surface: the upside-down gives an identical result because the stitch occurs in reversed sequence.

If you want to make the chain look like the upper surface of the ring—the more attractive side in the presence of picots—you can do so by working it in reversed sequence, one purl, one plain. In many patterns some rings have to be reversed, on account of their position in the design (notably the Wheel). By altering the stitch sequence they can be made to appear as if worked right side up, if you consider this to be an advantage.

Altering the sequence can mean more than merely reversing the order of plain and purl. For example it is possible to use one kind only for the entire piece.

The twist

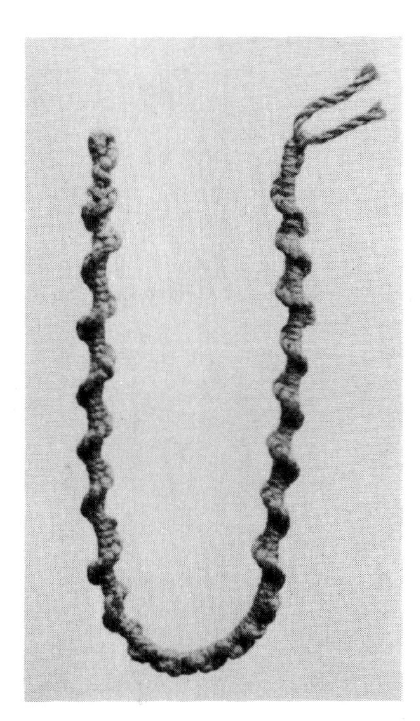

Fig. II 3

When you were learning the stitch, you practised the first half before you learned the second. You were warned that if you made too many the chain would begin to twist on itself, but that when you worked the two alternately, this tendency would be counteracted. If you had persisted for some length, the twist would develop to such an extent that it would produce a distinct arrangement of its own. A tight chain of all plain will show a pronounced ridge encircling the running thread rising in an anti-clockwise direction, left to right. One worked of all purl will cause the direction of the ridge to reverse: it will be clockwise, right to left, the mirror image of the first. Both are shown in Fig. II. **3**, where the two twists are employed to make a U-shaped form. The short base of the U is worked in Node stitch.

It must be admitted that the cotton at present obtainable is not so co-operative in this respect as formerly. The clockwise twist does appear fairly easily, but the anti-clockwise does not, and a great deal of persuasion with the fingers is required to make it do so. These forms, however, are rather of a freak nature and seldom appear, if ever, in English patterns, but modern Italian patterns use both rings and chains in lively combination, worked rather loosely so that the chains are more pliable.

Node stitch

This is an original style derived from the twist. It combines both, taking two similar stitches alternately. The following two of the opposite kind immediately counteract the twist, which has already begun, but not only do they counteract, they start a new twist in the reverse direction. The effect is a very small extrusion or node appearing alternately on both sides of the chain which is straight. In other words, the chain shows recurring interrupted twists. A line of node stitch takes on exciting and unexpected qualities, out of proportion to its simplicity. Owing to its construction it requires a different style of formula and diagram. Its technique comprises Part III.

The Josephine knot

This is a very small ring of eight or ten *single* stitches all of one kind, plain or purl. They lie very compactly, making a neat little rosette. The stitches must be at rather slack tension, and the running thread pulled up not too tightly, but completely, to make a perfect circle. It is named after Napoleon's empress, and was much used in early French patterns. It has been described as the Josephine Ring, and also Picot: this last I consider misleading. It is described here under the Stitch, and not under the Ring, as it involves a special sequence of stitches. It is too small to show by itself, but is illustrated as an ornament to a chain, which usually carries it, on p. 78.

The locking stitch

This is a suggested name for a single stitch—plain or purl—that is incomplete, namely, unturned, so that the tension of the running thread is broken at this point. It is used in designs where the tension must be interrupted so that a succeeding portion does not influence the stitches preceding it, as in a chain with right angles. To make it, on arrival at the required position, leave a stitch unturned: leave two unturned if the angle is external. Then continue as usual. The stitch of course is unnoticeable: you only see the effect it has on the piece. A chain with right angles is shown in Fig. II. 4.

The locking stitch allows a chain to start with a loop, perhaps its most important application, described in the section on the Chain (p. 66).

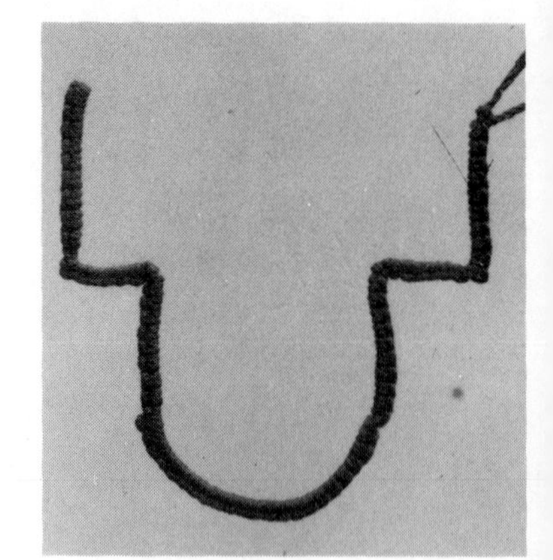

Fig. II 4

TENSION

The run-out line

This is an unashamed stunt. Its effect depends entirely on the tension of the running thread. A chain is worked in the normal way, with the stitches rather tight. When you have worked an inch or more, hold the start and with the fingers stretch the stitches apart—i.e. run them out along the shuttle thread as far as they will go. They will go surprisingly far for stitches supposed to be tight. The chain, instead of slightly curving with the stitches uppermost, now curls in the opposite direction, stitches inside, in a very decided fashion.

Fig. II. 5 shows a chain starting with twenty doubles at light tension, which are held by a locking stitch. Another twenty doubles are worked, but 'run-out', so curving in the opposite direction. This section can be laid in any direction you wish, as it is now very pliable. The two parts of the chain are worked identically. Only tension in the first, and lack of it in the second, is responsible for this rather curious effect.

If not run out completely, the chain will form a dead straight line—straighter than a chain of normal tension can. This can be used for outlining other work, for example, a strip of single pearl tatting, as shown in the lettering on the Greek plaque (facing p. 64).

THE RING

The ring is resistant to further manipulation. Its size, the number of picots it carries, and its position in a design, have been fully exploited. The three models to follow were all developed in the early 1800's, and are expressive of the state of tatting at that time.

A normal ring, being a closed circle, brings the thread back to where it started, which is not a progressive movement.

Fig. II 5

When it was the only shape known, great ingenuity was shown in carrying the thread to another position from which to start the next, some distance from the first. This is the theme of the first two examples, which use different methods. Although long obsolete, both can be adapted to modern use.

If a ring is not drawn up completely, leaving a stretch of unworked thread between start and finish, the object of getting away from the start is roughly achieved. In very early books they appear in succession, rather large and spaced apart, forming a line. Very small, say of only three doubles, the rings almost touching one another, they made a neat little string, used in fine lace work. These are returning in some modern patterns. I have used (invisibly) a medium size in the pattern for wheat. A practical application of this so-called 'half-ring' is to use the larger size as loops for buttonholes.

Buttonhole loops

Making and inserting loops of any kind for something to wear is not elementary dressmaking at any time, but tatted loops are simple to make compared with strips of fabric, and if done well they do give a professional finish.

To make them, first select the buttons, which are usually small. Sew one down on a piece of material, and work an experimental half-ring to determine the size of the loop it will need. It is a help if you start and end the ring with five doubles, making a small picot at these points to serve as balance marks.

The row of loops will be sewn to a fold of the fabric. The picots can rest on the inside of the edge (out of sight) or just outside it, where they will make a neat little decoration. When estimating the size, do not include the five doubles, which will not be free to pass round the button, but the *length* of the unworked thread (concealed) will. Next decide on the distance between the loops: this depends on the spacing you want. They should be fairly close together.

Assume you are making five loops, ½ inch apart, as in the model. Make a half-ring, with twenty doubles between picots, thus: 5ds P 20ds P 5ds. Draw up (partly) to the required size: the stitches must be tight, and the loop kept well open.

Leave a space of ½ inch and work the next ring. If the space is longer than you intended it does not matter, as the surplus will be out of sight, but it must not be less.

When the strip of rings is complete, tack firmly to a fold of the material, the picot (if liked) just showing. Lay a second folded strip over the first, edges corresponding, and tack it down very securely. Machine down in a straight line as near the edge as possible. The model shows the strip with the upper fold covering the first three loops, then turned back to show the remainder tacked in position.

Fig. II 6

This is not the only way of inserting the loops, and in fact for hand-made buttonholes machine top-stitching should not show. This can be avoided, but the method given, which concentrates on the tatting, rather than the style of the blouse opening, is simpler to demonstrate using one illustration. Shown in Fig. II. 6.

The loops can of course be used elsewhere, as a front fastening on a matching belt, cuffs, and a pocket flap. They can be worked in the usual cotton, or with double silk threads for a silk blouse. For a jacket, use double threads of thick cotton.

Passing the thread behind

Another method of getting the thread away from the start of

Fig. II 7

Fig. II 7a

a closed ring was to pass it behind the ring just worked, to lie upon one side of it, to emerge from a chosen picot into which it was knotted. The simplest form is a strip of nine (or more) rings, which can be drawn into a circle. It is shown in Fig. II. 7. Its reverse side, showing the passage of the thread, is shown in Fig. II. 7a.

As a variation they could be set at an angle, which, repeated in reverse, formed an edging of zig-zag appearance.

The Zig-zag

This is a pattern of Riego's, originally described as the Vandyke, which signified 'pointed strips of lace' as portrayed by the painter Van Dyck. Since many patterns contain Vandykes, it is impracticable to use it as a title for one. It is slightly revised and offered under the title of Zig-Zag.

Description: three rings form a line inclining downwards towards the right. The third also forms the first of three sloping upwards, also towards the right. The first and third rings stand vertically, upwards and downwards respectively. Between them lies a ring diagonally placed, behind which the thread passes (unseen) to bring it into position for the next vertical. The repetition of the design consists of four rings: of the pattern, two.

Construction: the rings are identical in size, all carrying positions for ten picots two doubles apart, therefore consisting of twenty doubles. As the ring starts and ends with two doubles, a tenth picot is absent, as it cannot form at a junction. Each ring makes a normal join to the one before it.

The verticals carry seven free picots, the diagonals six, three a side. The remainder of the picots (to make up the ten places) are either concerned with the join, or are engaged by knotting the thread into them (thus they are no longer free) or their position is occupied by the thread leaving a ring. The work is reversed every two rings, which accounts for the change in direction and also allows the same formula to be used by all. The only difference between them is in the way they start—from a free-standing thread or a knotted-in picot. The starts do not disturb the actual construction of the ring. The diagonals start from a free thread as it leaves a vertical: the verticals start from a picot on the diagonal through which the thread is knotted. The starting ring—in the model an upper vertical—is slightly different as there is no previous ring to which it can join. It therefore carries one extra free picot, making a total of eight. Always check the number of picots, free and engaged, before you draw up a ring: it saves many mistakes.

Working instructions: Starting ring: 2ds 9(P 2ds). Standard ring (all others) 2ds J, 8(2ds P) 2ds. The join is to the nearest picot on the previous ring.

Work the starting ring and pull up tightly. Work the diagonal (standard) starting in the normal way close to the previous ring, not quite touching it. Complete the formula and pull up. This pair is presented the right way up, as worked.

You now have to get the thread into position for the lower vertical. Carry it behind the diagonal to lie upon one side of it, it does not matter which, as the distance it will cover is the same either way round. Leave plenty of slack or it will show from the front, and knot it into the fourth picot from the join.

You are now ready to start the next couple, for which turn the work over to the reverse side. For the lower vertical, repeat the standard ring, starting close up to the knotted picot. Then work the next diagonal, starting with the free thread. On completion of this pair, pass the thread this time on the surface of the ring, as you have been working on the reverse side.

Turn back again to right side up and start the next pair with the upper vertical. Continue for as long as necessary, ending with a vertical, upper or lower, whichever you need. The model is shown in Fig. II. 8, and a working diagram in Fig. II. 8a.

The diagram should clarify these instructions. The picots concerned with joins and knotting are drawn in as exaggerated loops: inside the latter a small cross + signifies a knot. Arrows outside the rings show the direction in which the ring is worked, thus indicating when the work is reversed.

Fig. II 8

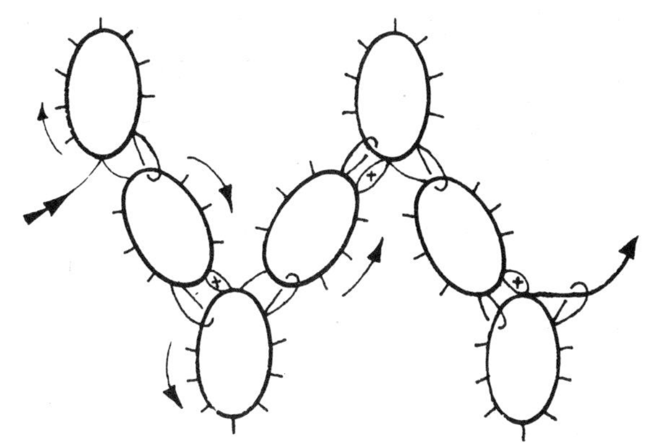

Fig. II 8a

In spite of the long explanation of the pattern, once understood it is easy to memorise, and when you have made one vertical and one diagonal with their appropriate starts, the rest is repetition. It is a good piece to pick up at odd moments on this account.

For a bolder effect make the rings larger, so that there are positions for twelve picots instead of ten. The piece can be drawn into a circle, or oval, but it will not turn a corner.

Applications: it is very suitable for children's clothes, laid on the hem of a little dress, and attractive on cuffs and belt. Two rows, straight across, or laid diagonally, are effective on a fabric bag. A row, straight, with another beneath it so that the verticals touch, makes a bold wide band enclosing diamond shapes. This could be repeated indefinitely, forming a rather openwork allover piece. If to stand independently, then the second row may join by its verticals to those opposite, at their centre picots.

The Lozenge

The Lozenge, though primitive, as it belongs to a very early period, is an advanced style of work, using both shuttle and needle. Fine pieces of intricate design, composed of lozenges and circles, remain in museums and private hands as a memorial to the ingenuity of their time. The method of making them probably never appeared in print, but was handed down from one worker to another as was then the custom. Its originator is unknown: it is likely that it preceded Riego. No one would use it now, unless they specialised in old patterns, but it would seem a pity to let it pass into oblivion. The result is more lace-like than any succeeding style of tatting. It is firm but pliable, retaining its shape, while its very feel on handling is one of delicacy. This desirable effect is due to the fact that the normal join had not yet been invented. Joins of one ring to another were made with a needle, as were strips of rings one to another. Ovals were thus built up to compose the principal units in broad lengths of lace. A comparatively simple Lozenge is shown in Fig. II. 9.

Fig. II 9

It is basically a medallion, enclosed space type, worked in three rounds. These are: the centre-piece, a surrounding row of rings, and an outer row. A detailed pattern is not presented, the main object being to show the special method of joining with the needle, but without an illustration the description would be unconvincing.

The centre-piece is a short strip of rings, two large and six small, carrying picots, and brought round so that first and last meet. The interior space thus formed is 'filled', or occupied, by twisting the two thread ends together, carried on needles, giving an elastic and pliable 'core'. For convenience this needlework is best left until the rest is complete.

The surrounding row of rings consists of a strip of twelve,

Plate I *A plaque with the traditional Greek Orthodox monogram signifying 'Christ the Victor.' It is worn either on a shawl (correctly a 'veil') or on the orphreys of a priest's vestment. Commissioned by the Rev. Kyriacos Korniotis for the parish of the Transfiguration of Christ, Welling, Kent.*

Plate II *Thistles and Corn. The techniques used are described at the end of Part II.*

carrying seven rather large picots, adjoining. The first ring leaves about 18 inches of thread behind it. A space of thread is left between each ring, roughly the length of two picots. On completion of the strip, cut off the shuttle and take the starting end on a needle, passing it up through the first picot of the second ring, and the last picot of the first, in that order. Then behind both, and the space of thread connecting the rings. These three are knotted firmly together, making a tight little bundle at midway.

Then carry the needle thread on, to knot into the base of the second ring and so be in a position to continue until the last ring meets and joins with the first. The threads from both shuttle and needle will now meet. The small inset shows two rings so joined, the distance between them exaggerated, with extra long picots for the join.

For a practice piece work a strip in this manner, standing alone: but for the Lozenge, pick up with the needle the picots on the first round (centre-piece) as you proceed, knotting them into the base of the round you are working on. The shape is now a well-defined oval. The external round consists of sixteen rings of nine picots, and rather longer spaces, constructed as before, joining to the centre picot of the rings of the preceding round. Once you have become accustomed to the needle this is quicker to work than it appears.

It is hoped that someone will restore life to this long obsolete method. Several Lozenges can be arranged into a number of attractive shapes.

THE CHAIN

'In all the notices I can find there seems to be no idea that anything but circles, ovals, or adaptations of circles, can be made. But with two shuttles and an inventive brain, there is no end to the designs that can be invented'. Such was Lady Hoare's comment on the state of tatting and publications of the period. The chain—the tatting discovery of the century—in 1864 had not been as enthusiastically received as it deserved. It was in fact largely neglected by the designers of the day. Lady Hoare's inventive brain, however, applied it to such effect that she opened up a new world, producing styles hitherto undreamed of. She still used what she then called 'single tatting' with one thread, but she now developed 'double tatting' with two shuttles. (These titles are no longer current). The second shuttle was nevertheless not put to its fullest use: it simply supplied a second thread as an auxiliary. Now, more than a century since its discovery, the chain is exploited still further, and a few more added. Some are revivals of methods once popular but now discarded, perhaps as being over-elaborate, but they produce interesting effects which no other method can.

Starting with a 'picot'

(this is an application of the locking stitch)

Modern work often requires a chain to start with a picot. A true picot needs a double stitch to precede it. This can be dispensed with by making use of the starting loop, locking it to produce a 'false' picot.

With a continuous thread arrange a loop under the thumb as in starting an ordinary chain. Holding it tightly, make an unturned purl stitch, leaving the loop the size required for the 'picot'. Follow with an ordinary purl. These two stitches count as one double. Continue the chain.

This is not the only way of making the loop, but the simplest to describe. With a large loop this is simple, you can see what you are doing, and you have the loop to hold on to. With a very small one, described as a 'Link-loop' ('Ll' in a formula) you have not, and the stitches are out of sight under the thumb. It is a help to put a pin in the loop, and make the first two stitches hard up against it. Leave the pin in until you have worked a short distance in ordinary sequence. Practise, making the loop in several sizes, large ones first, and eventually the smallest possible size, for an invisible join by other work, often to the start of the chain itself, to make a circle. A chain starting with a loop is shown in Fig. II. 10.

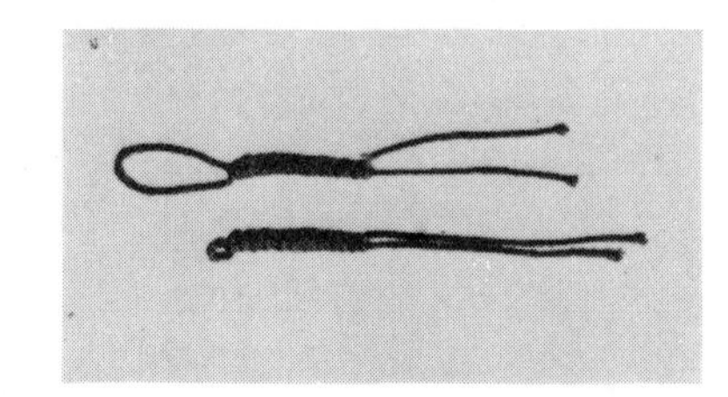

Fig. II 10

THE REVERSING CHAIN

This is a chain which reverses the direction of the stitches at required positions. There are two methods of doing this. (1) Overturning the chain at a given point so that the stitches lie on the opposite side, and (2) using a second working shuttle, exchanging the two at arranged intervals.

Method 1a: turning at a join to a picot

A model built up from Vandykes and scallops is chosen

because it can be applied in a number of ways. It is taken from an Australian pattern book, where it provided an upstanding edge to a tea-cosy, covered with tatting on both sides, the edging following the seams of the cosy.

Description: a one-round edging, the whole on one pair of threads. A Vandyke alternates with a scallop, separated by an intermediate ring. The scallop carries the reversing chain.

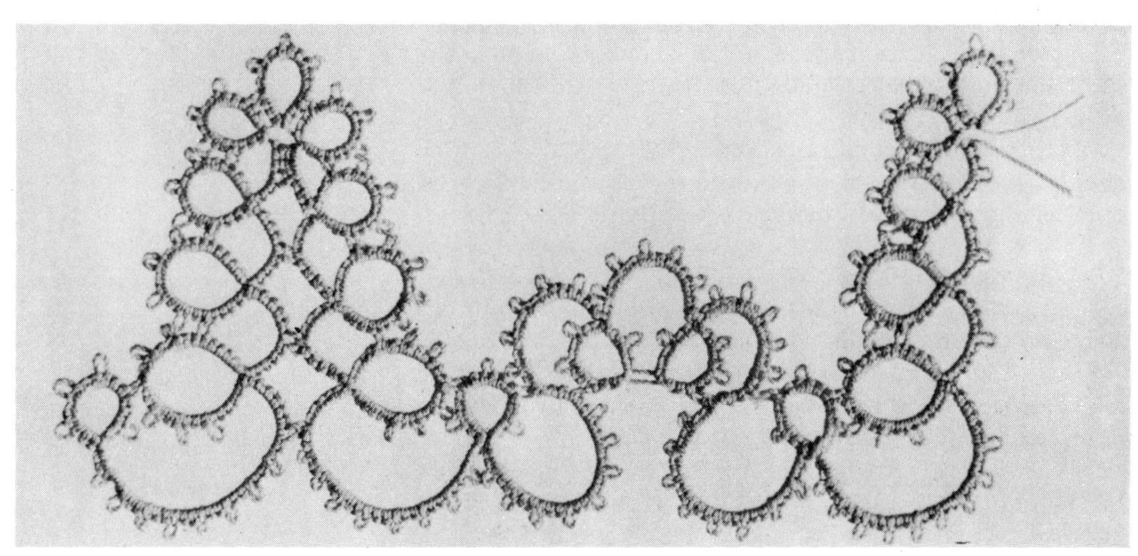

Fig. II 11

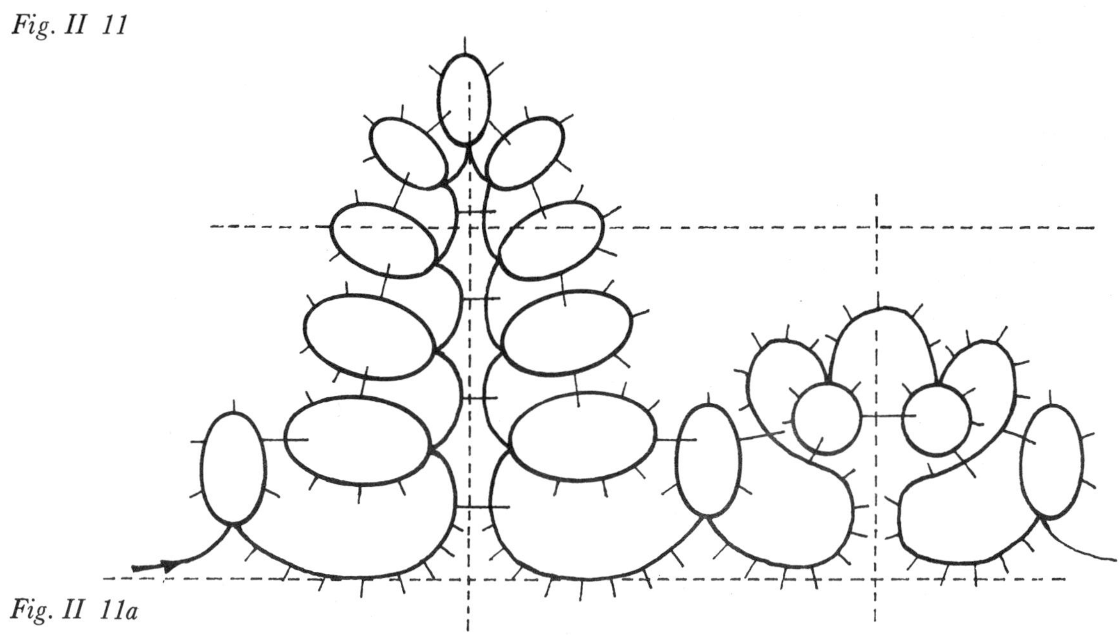

Fig. II 11a

Construction: The Vandyke is formed by an ascending series (left side) of rings and chains, to which is joined a similar series, descending (right side) worked in reverse order. The first and last chains of the figure are very long, joining to the intermediate ring on either side. The ascending rings decrease in size as they approach the top, which is a trefoil whose rings are equal. They are reduced by losing one double in the first and last sections of each ring, and by reducing the number of picots they carry (in the first three rings only). There are seven in the first, six in the second, and five in the third and in the trefoil. Joins, (two to a ring) are counted as picots, so a ring carrying positions for seven picots will show five free. The three chains connecting the rings also lose one double on either side of their centre picot. The reductions are very slight but they produce a well-proportioned figure.

The scallop consists of a pair (left and right) of reversing chains, a short chain across the top, and two identical rings facing downwards within. The picots on all rings and chains are three doubles apart, except in those which are increasing or reducing in size. The model and a working drawing are shown in Figs. II 11 and 11a.

Working instructions: start with an intermediate ring: 3ds 5(P 3ds).
The Vandyke: 1st (long chain) 9 (3ds P) 6ds.
1st ring (lowest): 6ds 3(P 3ds) J to 4th picot of intermediate ring, 3(3ds P) 6ds.
2nd chain: 5ds P 5ds.
2nd ring: 5ds, J to last picot of last ring, 5(3ds P) 5ds.
3rd chain: 4ds P 4ds.
3rd ring: 4ds, J as before, 4(3ds P) 4ds.
4th chain: 3ds P 3ds.
The trefoil: 3 rings, worked close together, joined, each of 5 picots, 3ds apart.
After the trefoil, start the descending series.
1st chain: 3ds, J to the chain opposite, 3ds.
1st ring: 4ds, J to last ring of trefoil, 4(3ds P) 4ds.
2nd chain: 4ds, J to chain opposite, 4ds.
2nd ring: 5ds, J to last picot of last ring: 5(3ds P) 5ds.
3rd chain: 5ds, J as before, 5ds.
3rd ring: 6ds, J to last picot of last ring: 6(3ds P) 6ds.
The long chain: 6ds, J to last picot of chain opposite, follow with 8 free picots 3ds apart, finishing with 3ds.
This concludes the Vandyke. Continue with an intermediate

ring, joining at second picot-position to the 4th picot of the last ring of the Vandyke.

The scallop: the two reversing chains are not exactly replicas, but this is unavoidable owing to the order in which the rings and chains are worked, for you can only reverse (by this method) at an existing picot, to which the chain joins.

The left side chain is no problem. It joins into a picot on the previous intermediate ring, and reverses (i.e. is turned over) at this point. For the right side chain, however, the next intermediate ring does not yet exist, so it must join to the nearest picot in its path, a picot on the second ring, which is present. The two joins therefore are not perfectly balanced, but this is virtually unnoticeable.

Furthermore, this pattern is exactly as the original described, but the scallop does not lie very comfortably—it is too cramped and its two long chains at the base are too near together, tending to overlap. To avoid this, make the picot on the first ring to which the second ring joins, much longer, so that the two halves of the scallop are further apart. This is not recorded in the pattern, or represented in the model. If you follow the diagram you will see which picot to enlarge. The result will be a better balanced figure.

Proceeding from the intermediate ring, work an ascending chain carrying nine picots facing down, ending with 3ds. Join into the 4th picot of the intermediate: the auxiliary will be on the wrong side, but this will help to pull the chain over. Continue the chain, but with the picots facing the opposite way. Work five picots, ending with 3ds. This concludes the left reversing chain. Reverse the work.

1st ring: 5 picots, 3ds apart, joining its centre picot position to the picot before the reversing join on the lower curve. Reverse.

2nd ring: 3ds P 3ds, J to 4th picot of first ring: 3(3ds P) 3ds. Reverse. For the descending chain: 6(3ds P) 3ds, J to 3rd picot of 2nd ring, reversing at this point. Follow with 8(3ds P) 3ds.

This concludes the scallop and one repetition of the piece. The scallop will not settle into its position until the next intermediate ring is in place. Work it, joining to the last picot before the reversing join on the upper curve of the chain. Continue with the next Vandyke.

Application of the piece: this edging can lie in a straight line, or be curved slightly in either direction. Curved it can form a collar to a blouse—either back or front fastening. It can ornament the line of a yoke, placed from shoulder to shoulder (curved) or across from one armhole to another (straight). A back fastening is preferable, but a short and inconspicuous front opening is possible in both cases. It can form turn-back cuffs on long or short sleeves. Two Vandykes placed in opposition to one another, joined at the centre picots of the long chains, make an attractive simulated buckle, sewn to a fabric belt, which should have a side fastening. Other selected edgings can perform most of these duties, provided they can make the appropriate curve. Whatever position it occupies, it must be the right size for the garment. The size of the thread determines the number of motifs you need for a given length, which of course depends on the size of the blouse and in the case of a collar the neck opening.

Overturning during progress: second example of Method 1

The second example shows a turn while the chain is in progress between joins, demonstrated in a strip of work, both sides alike. With modification the strip can turn a corner. The ring at the corner is worked on a second shuttle, but without the corner, a straight strip can be worked on shuttle and ball. The whole is made on one pair of threads.

Strip with corner, Moorish style

A chain is made in the normal way, the 'reverse' being obtained by turning it over sharply with the fingers at the point required, which is marked by a small picot—'turning picot'—tp in the formula. The join is always to the facing picot on the curve opposite, as the model shows. The formula for a strip, starting as the model, with the last half of an upper curve, left side, is as follows:
10ds P 5ds tp 5ds 2(P 10ds) P 5ds tp 5ds 5ds J, 2(10ds P) 5ds tp 5ds.

The starting section is rather long because four picots have to be made before a join is possible. The following portion between brackets is the repetition. This is short, as both upper and lower edges are alike. Work some straight strips to practise the turns and to acquire even tension. The chain lies better if it is not actually turned when you reach the tp, but when it is necessary to do so—on arrival at a join, when you must turn to get the auxiliary on the appropriate side.

The straight strip can be used on blouse or jacket, with the corner if the design requires it. It can be eased round a neckline, or a stand-up collar, attached to a short cape, which it can also outline. Two rows, side by side, joined by their ornamental picots, can be laid on a belt.

The corner

A working formula is given for the corner, but before attempting it look at the model, Fig. II. 12, and check it with the description which should make the model easier to follow.

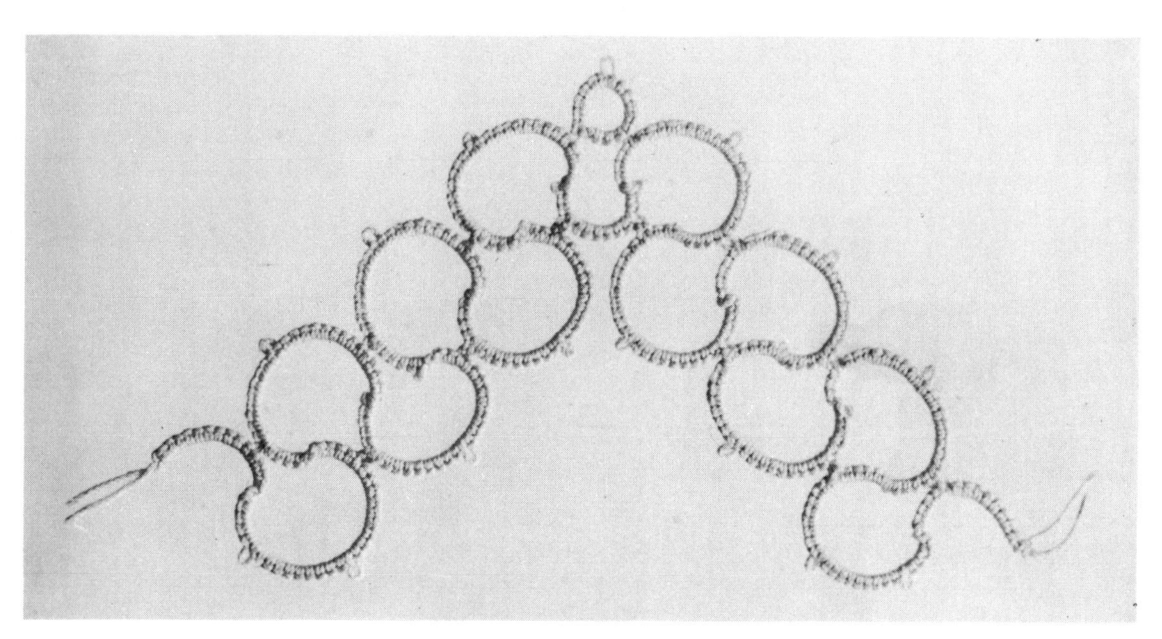

Fig. II 12

Flask and cork

The corner includes a little flask with a cork, inserted between two strips at right angles. To accommodate the flask, and make the turn, slight adjustments are necessary to both upper and lower neighbouring curves. The first variation starts from the ornamental picot on the lower curve, left side. The normal joining picot is omitted, but another replaces it a little higher up, to which the flask will join. The tp remains in its usual position.

The upper curve is worked normally until the position of its right side joining picot is reached: then it throws out a ring (the cork) as described in the section on the second working shuttle. After the ring the chain continues downwards (with the tp) to form the left side of the flask, joining to the new picot on the lower curve. The base of the flask follows, and the ascent (right side) which is the reverse of the left, just worked. The flask is concluded by joining into the last picot of the cork. The new strip starts by continuing the chain normally for the upper curve. The following lower curve joins into the remaining picot on the flask, and continues until it reaches the lower ornamental picot. This concludes the corner modification.

To work the corner: Abbr: UC=Upper Curve: LC=Lower Curve.

The ring, being on a second shuttle, is given separately, to prevent confusion with the chain. Its first picot is ornamental: the second, small, for joining.

The ring: 2 (6ds P) 3ds.

The chain: starting from the ornamental picot on a lower curve, work as follows: 12ds P 3ds tp 5ds J, (to UC): 10ds P 10ds. Now work the ring.

Continue the chain thus: 5ds tp 3ds J, (to LC) 7ds P 3ds tp 5ds J. This join is to the ring, completing the flask.

Continue with 2(10ds P) 5ds tp 3ds J, (to flask) 12ds. Follow with P 10ds, thus returning to the original formula for the strip.

A medallion

A strip can be modified to form a circle by making the upper curve larger and the lower one smaller, using six repetitions tightly worked. The result is a series of large flasks facing inwards, alternating with small flasks facing out. This is quick to make. The repetition of the pattern, starting with the base of a small flask, is as follows: 10ds P 7ds tp 7ds P 30ds P 7ds tp 7ds J to small flask.

Start with a link-loop at the head of a chain at midway in the base of a small flask, where you will finish. Work the first repetition, then follow with the second, but prior to making the 30 doubles for the upper curve, *join* to the picot already made. Similarly, at the end of the sixth and last upper curve, join to the picot carried on the first, instead of making one. This should be clear from the illustration, Fig. II. 13.

The joins are from curve to curve as before, but for better proportions a cork (two sizes) inserted in the necks of the flasks makes a much more graceful piece. The corks are on a

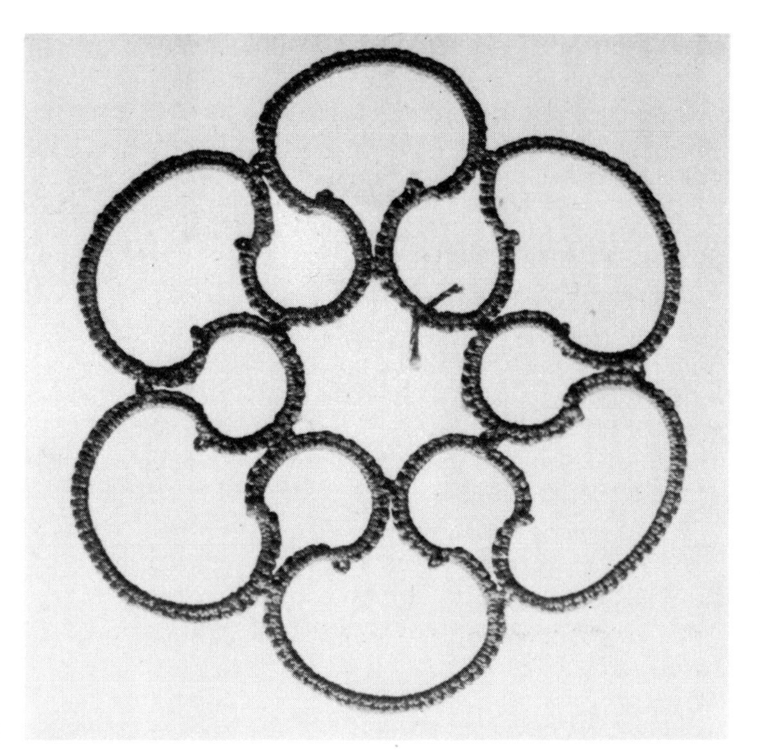

Fig. II 13

Fig. II 14

second shuttle. Fig. II. 14 shows a lampshade ornamented with a medallion so made, in No. 60 thread. The interior—a central ring and surrounding chain—was inserted after the flasks were worked. A matching edging decorates both edges of the shade.

Turning with two shuttles

The second method of turning, by using two shuttles, is not new. The result is perfectly flat, and would be considered better tatting, but it lacks the grace of the former method. An example is given in the Starfish, a small medallion of five repetitions, with a picot at the centre (correctly a link-loop). Each of the five 'arms' is formed by a double scallop to give a half-moon effect. It is an advantage if you can work the stitch upside down, to avoid the constant reversing of the piece.

To work, start a chain with a link-loop, rather large. Its size can only be arrived at by trial and error, depending on the thread, and tension. Work twelve doubles for the outer curve of an arm. Change shuttles, thus reversing the direction of the stitches, and work ten doubles for the inner. Tuck the two chains closely together, the tip well rounded. Now back at the link-loop, join into it.

Again change shuttles: work four more arms, each joining to the loop. They will not settle comfortably until the last is in. Finish by tying into the loop.

By using two shuttles you can, for variety, take threads of two colours, and also make the inner curve of finer thread, which will take more stitches. The centre should be a small open circle, with no part of the loop showing. It takes some practice. There are simpler ways of demonstrating this form of reversing. It could have been used in the Vandyke and Scallop edging, to its advantage. The Starfish is shown in Fig. II. 15.

Fig. II 15

CROSSING ONE LINE WITH ANOTHER: OVER AND UNDER JOINS

I do not think, in correct tatting, that a chain has ever been passed over or under another Since the work is expected to lie flat, such an arrangement would be unacceptable to workers of traditional styles. A crossed line, however, does make new arrangements possible, as the examples show.

A line may cross another without actually joining to it, in a position where they will be undisturbed. The body of the Thistle in Plate III is made in this way, the outline of the flower holding them in place, but where rigidity is necessary one chain must join into a picot carried on another—usually a distant part of itself, previously worked. Such joins are shown in the Celtic Cross, referred to later.

In a crossing requiring a join, both chains are involved. One is Passive, carrying the picots: the other is Active, joining to them. According to the way the Passive lies, the picot will be either on the near side, in relation to the approaching Active, or beyond it. In either position the Active can join into it, passing over or under the Passive, whichever the pattern requires. Irrespective of the position of the picot, near or far, and the type of join, the procedure of making the join is the same in all cases. The auxiliary thread is drawn *up* through the picot and pulled *very* tightly after the shuttle thread has passed through it. The picot must be very small, to hold the active chain in place. An underjoin to a chain where the picot is on the far side is the easiest to start with. It is used in the Cord of Loops.

The Cord of Loops

The join here is straightforward, but it is combined with an overturned chain, which gives the effect of a real chain of links.

Construction: (for short lengths of chain, not exceeding six inches). Work a chain with a link-picot at the start, carrying link-picots at regular intervals (in the model twelve doubles). End with twenty-four doubles, omitting the last picot. This is the Passive. From now on it is Active, for it will work back and around the Passive, forming underjoins with its picots. The joins will appear as over and under alternately, as the work is reversed before each (except the first).

Bring the now Active chain round towards you to form the first link, the threads carried up to and under the Passive, and make an underjoin to the nearest picot. Work the next section of twelve doubles. At present the stitches on both chains are facing inwards, towards one another. Overturn both chains at the join so that they face out.

Reverse the work, which will bring you into position for making the next join.

Repeat the last four motions thus: underjoin to nearest

picot—twelve doubles—overturn both chains—reverse the work. This is the repetition of the Active chain.

Finish by joining into the link-picot at the start. The model, Fig. II. 16, shows five loops and two picots waiting to be connected.

Practise some short strips until the motions are familiar. Equal tension in the two chains is of great importance.

A long line of loops should be worked with two separate chains, each with shuttle and ball, which gives much better control. Start as usual but stop after the fourth or fifth picot. With a new pair of threads for the Active chain, join into the link-loop at the start, twelve doubles, underjoin, exactly as in the short strip. Work three or four links, then pick up the Passive, and continue with it, always following with the Active about two links behind. A cord of any length can be made in the manner.

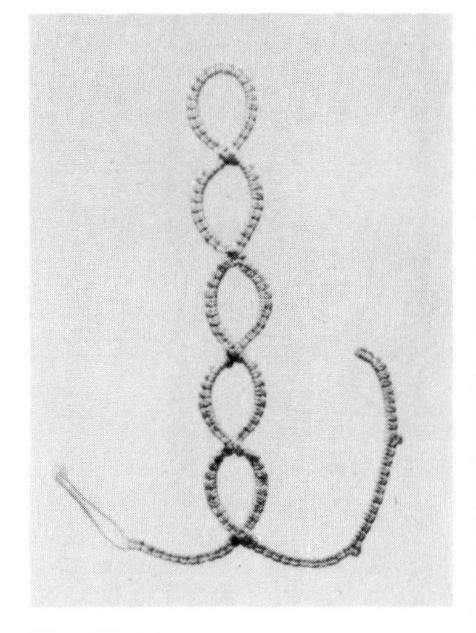

Fig. II 16

Application of the cord: this is a useful and practical formation. It can lie straight, turn a right angle with very little adjustment, or be curved in either direction to form a circle. The loops can be any size, and carry picots at any point for ornament or for joining. It makes a neat finish to a tailored garment, for example on a collar or cuffs. It should be sewn on the fabric a short distance from the edge. Two parallel rows can be laid down the front of a buttoned blouse, on either side of the buttonholes. It is effective round the edges of a straight-hung jacket.

In more elaborate constructions, with many joins, the size of the apertures is of great importance. The design may require the joins to be close together, forming apertures through which the shuttle needs to, but cannot, pass. This entails threading both shuttle and auxiliary on either sewing or fine netting needles: both must pass through. With a sewing needle you can pass directly through the picot, instead of picking up a loop of the auxiliary. The result is smoother and flatter.

The Celtic Cross

Originally carved in stone, was made in this manner. Its description would be: 'A geometrical design of four repetitions, represented by an all-chain medallion, enclosed space centre. Over and under joins alternate throughout, and the whole is worked on one pair of threads'. This is an advanced piece of work, requiring needles, unless made on a much bigger scale, when shuttles can be used. Directions for working are not given. Shown in Fig. II. 17.

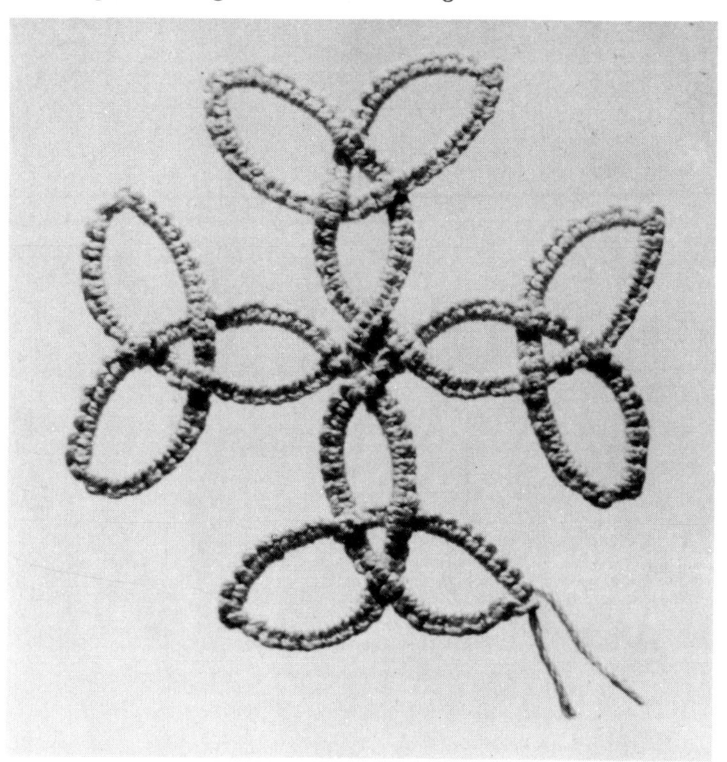

Fig. II 17

The mock ring

The mock ring is a suggested name for a chain brought round into a circle or oval, giving the appearance of a true ring, over which it has several advantages. It can carry a second working shuttle: it can substitute for a real ring which is too large to draw up. Two examples are given. In old French patterns the mock ring often replaced the central ring in a medallion, carrying, instead of picots, small ordinary rings to which an ensuing round joined. By making the chain all on the one running thread and throwing out the rings on a second shuttle, the circle is near perfect, and tension is under control. Such a medallion would be classed as an enclosed space formed by a chain, although of course it is apparently a ring. The second example shows a mock ring carrying three Josephine picots. The two are shown in Figs. II. 18 and 19, side by side.

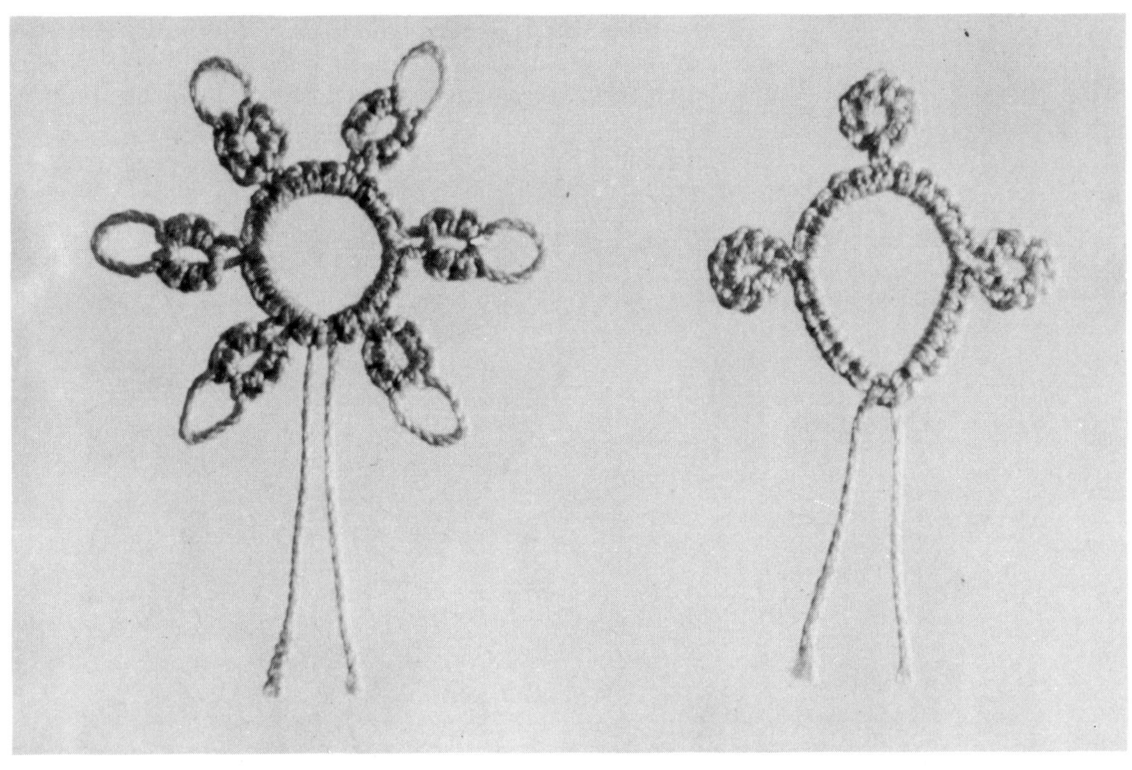

Fig. II 18 *Fig. II 19*

If the mock ring substitutes for a centrally placed ring in a pattern, and is required to carry precisely spaced picots to be joined by other work, the space occupied by the join of start to finish must be taken into account. The starting loop must be as small as possible and a single stitch or more subtracted from either the first or the last section, or both, so that the sections between picots are equal in length. This is more important than working the correct number of stitches.

Alternatively, if the mock ring is not too large, allow the starting loop—a very large one unlocked—eventually to telescope. Keep it open while working. After a few stitches pull the loop out so that you can carry it on your third finger in case of an accident. When complete, pass the shuttle through the loop and pull gently, easing the stitches along until the loop disappears. See that the tension is tight and even, all round, first and last stitches lying closely together. The two thread ends lie flat, both outside. It makes a perfect circle, better in fact than a real ring. The first mock ring to be described above was made in this manner. Notice how neatly the emerging threads lie. Precise workers will appreciate this rather special technique.

Some further arrangements

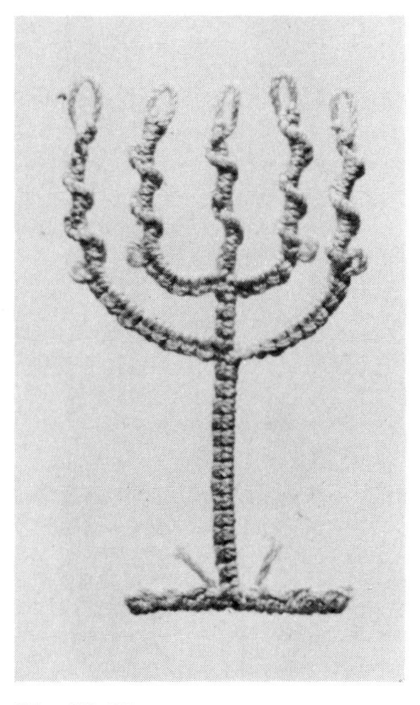

Fig. II 20

These are not the only methods of exploiting the chain, and a brief reference is made to some others for which details are not given. It can, with a locking stitch, or a second shuttle, be broken up into sections to lie alongside one another, massed to form flat solid blocks, much used in Italian patterns. The little starfish has just two such sections, curved.

Flat solid circles can be made of a chain worked round on itself to form mats: large for a medallion, small for the centre of a flower.

A more elaborate arrangement, now obsolete, which I call the False Chain, is one worked with one thread only. It is the tatting stitch, but not made by the characteristic tatting movement. I have used it to produce 'blind ends' in modern patterns. The Branched Candlestick is an extreme example, all on one pair of threads, the candles being made on one thread alone. This is an advanced piece of work, with a picot at the head of a false chain worked with a Twist, shown in Fig. II. 20, as a demonstration of how versatile a chain can be.

THE PICOT

The two functions of the picot are to ornament, and to make connections with other parts of the work, evolved in that order. As ornament: the number of picots, and their length, tends to vary with the period. How many you use depends on the effect you want, and the kind of work you are doing. Short are more practical but for traditional lace-work in fine thread, long ones are more suitable.

As an instrument for joining: connections can be intentionally obvious with a large picot, or they may be as unobtrusive as possible. In this case they are very small, no larger than you need to pass a fine hook through, and I mean hook, and not part of the thicker shaft as well. These make a very close join with no movement, giving extra body to the piece. These are described as Link-picots, abbreviation Lp.

A modern use for the picot is to employ it as part of the structure of the work, described later. (see The Join, pp 89–90).

Measuring

To have control over the picot it must be made to an exact size, therefore it must be measured. The gauge may be an ordinary six-inch scale, or a row of pins, evenly spaced, the points set firm in the edge of a flat piece of wood. Taking one inch as a standard length, decide how many divisions you want it to contain. This depends on the kind of work you do, and the thickness of the thread.

Eighths of an inch are an average size for ordinary work: tenths or sixteenths for finer. These are usually marked on the scale. An important detail is the firm fixing of the scale to the edge of a table, so that you will not knock it out of position when you approach it. The board with pins has an advantage here.

To make a measured picot, say half an inch long before drawing up, work a plain stitch at slightly more than this distance (by eye) on the thread, and then hold the work up against the scale, the last double resting at the first pin, or the start of an inch on a scale. This pin, or point, is numbered 0. Slide the stitch back until it is opposite the half-inch mark. Then, withdrawing from the scale, taking care that the stitch has not slipped, make the following purl and slide the pair back into position. The picot should be the required size. If it is to be more than one inch in length, say $1\frac{1}{4}$ inches, the mark on the scale—or the number of the pin—would be, if written, Pin 10, and so on. This avoids fractions.

With practice, measuring can be quicker than expected. The following example, the Feather, is made entirely of graduated, measured picots. It involves an overturned chain, and starts with an ornamental Josephine knot, giving a neat finish.

The feather

The feather is a row of paired scallops facing up and down alternately. Each scallop is followed by two doubles, where the turn takes place. The first two consist of seven adjoining picots, the next two nine, and so on. Each pair is the same as the last plus one longer picot of the next size, and one extra

Plate III Rose Flamboyant, an advanced piece, $4\frac{1}{4}$ inches in diameter.

Plate IV   A group of shuttles from the author's collection.

of the same size as the previous long one, to keep the new long one in the centre. As the picots are adjoining, the difference in appearance of the upper and lower scallops, owing to reversing the work between each, would be rather obvious. To overcome this, all those made in reverse were worked in reverse sequence—1 purl, 1 plain—a refinement suitable for a demonstration piece. Shown in Fig. II. 21.

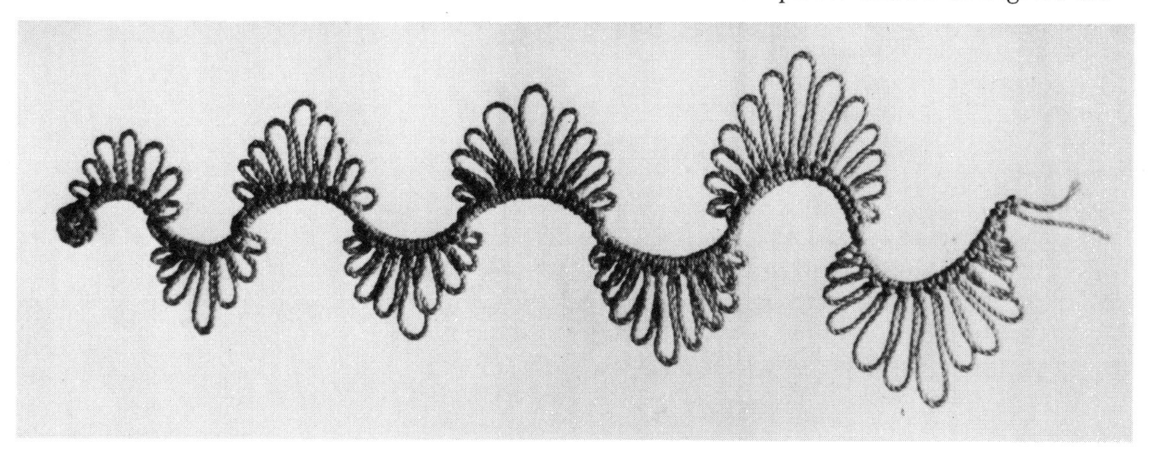

Fig. II 21

Small decorative pieces

These should be mounted under glass, accompanying other work. Rings of adjoining picots can be treated in various ways. They can be stretched out fully, pinned on a board, as in Fig. II. 22. The tips can be cut off, as in Fig. II. 23. The cut picots can be frayed, as in Fig. II. 24.

The frayed picot: fraying actually involves the end of a thread, not necessarily a cut picot, and might well be in the section on the thread, but it is more convenient to describe it here.

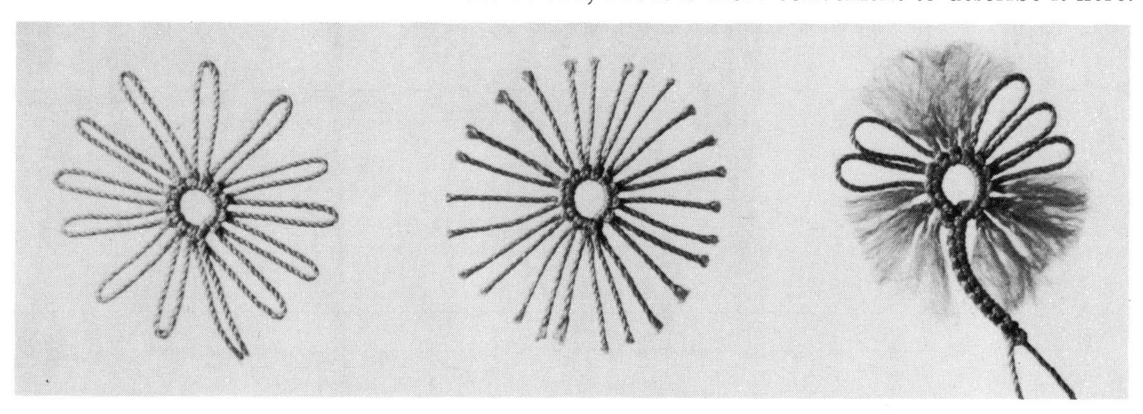

Fig. II 22 *Fig. II 23* *Fig. II 24*

To fray is tedious but effective. Cut through the picots, one at a time, and untwist one strand with the fingers: it will resolve into three. Separate each of these with a pin into its two components, which tease out completely. Smooth and stroke with the fingers: it will look like silk. To cut and fray all the picots on a ring of the above size, would make it look like a puff-ball—leave several uncut. When complete trim round with sharp scissors to get a neat circle—fraying causes the strands to lengthen.

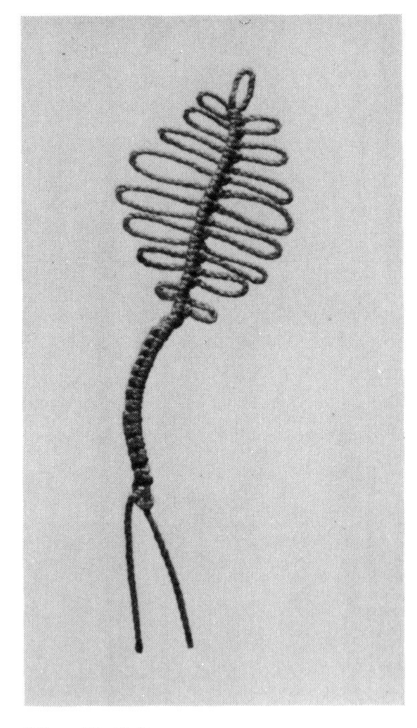

Fig. II 25

Pulled-over picots on a chain: these are used for forming primitive leaves. Work an ordinary chain starting with a locked loop about $\frac{1}{8}$ inch in length. Follow with adjoining picots, in pairs, increasing all the way down, or showing the longest at the centre. The model was worked in eighths, but sixteenths would give a larger leaf in better proportions. On completion slacken the chain slightly and pin out on a board, the picots on alternate sides. After wetting and resting, they will stay in position. The reverse side shows a well-defined rib. Shown in Fig. II. 25.

The twisted picot: these are used for shaping leaves and petals. A ring carries the required number: an outlining chain joins to them after they have been tightly twisted with the hook. The chain, which is anchored to link-picots on either side of the twist, is thus pulled into a heart shape. The length of the twisted picot, and the number of the stitches in the chain, are variables. Abbreviation: Tp.

The shamrock

This is a rigid, very precise leaf of three lobes carried on a ring. Make the ring, leaving enough thread to form a stalk. The twisted picot is $\frac{5}{8}$ inch, or Pin 5.

The ring: 1ds 3(Lp Tp) Lp. (Total 8ds). Pull up very tightly, reverse and work the stalk.

The enclosing chain: keeping the reverse side up, join with a new pair of threads into the Lp last worked (left side of piece). Work twelve doubles tight. Twist the long picot twice, and join the auxiliary into it. This will take much practice to avoid splitting the thread. Do not count this stitch.

Work another twelve doubles, join into the next Lp very tightly. This join must be flat, so the join is with the shuttle thread. Repeat for the remaining two petals, finishing at the first Lp. With the ring the wrong side up, as now presented, it appears smaller and neater. Fig. II. 26 shows a ring with stalk, waiting for the enclosing chain, and the finished leaf.

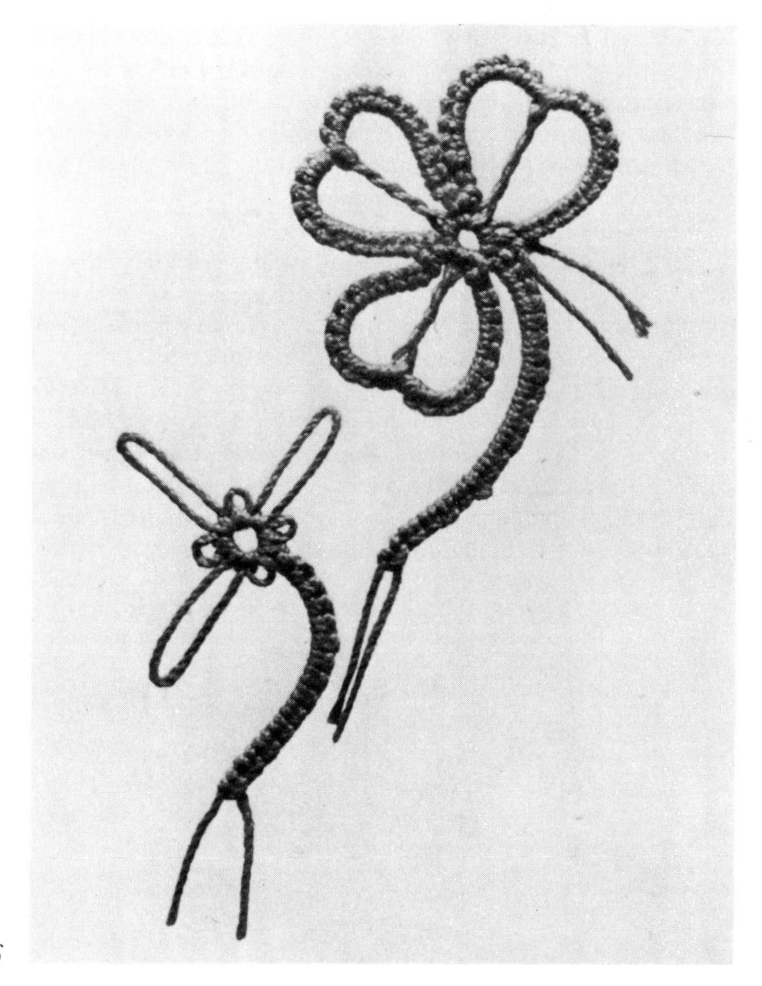

Fig. II 26

You cannot make twisted picots on a straight chain. They must be on a ring to balance the pull of the twist. This three-petalled piece is the best way of practising them.

The rose

This is a development of the shamrock. The ring is much larger, carrying five petals, and each petal has its own *pair* of link-picots. The distance between petals may vary. With one ds between the links, the petals will overlap slightly, suitable for a piece if worn in a buttonhole, when it carries a stalk. With two doubles between the petals, they will lie flat. This is essential if the rose is in the centre of a design to which other work joins. The model has two doubles between. The twisted picot is on Pin 7.

The formula for the ring is: 5(lds Lp Tp Lp 1ds) which will bring the two doubles between each petal. Work the ring, and draw it up, cut off the threads but leave them free for adjustment of tension. The surrounding chain sets better if worked on a new pair of threads.

Join the chain into any link-picot preceding a twist. Work eighteen doubles tight: join into the twist, giving it as many turns as you can, probably three. Repeat the eighteen doubles and join into the link on the ring, using the auxiliary. Make a locking stitch to break the tension, and join into the next link, ready for the next petal. Continue round until all the petals are formed. Pinch the petals into a heart shape. The foundation ring is unavoidably untidy: a little centre-piece should cover it. In the model a ring in node stitch, with rather long picots inside and out, is used. It is shown in Fig. II. 27.

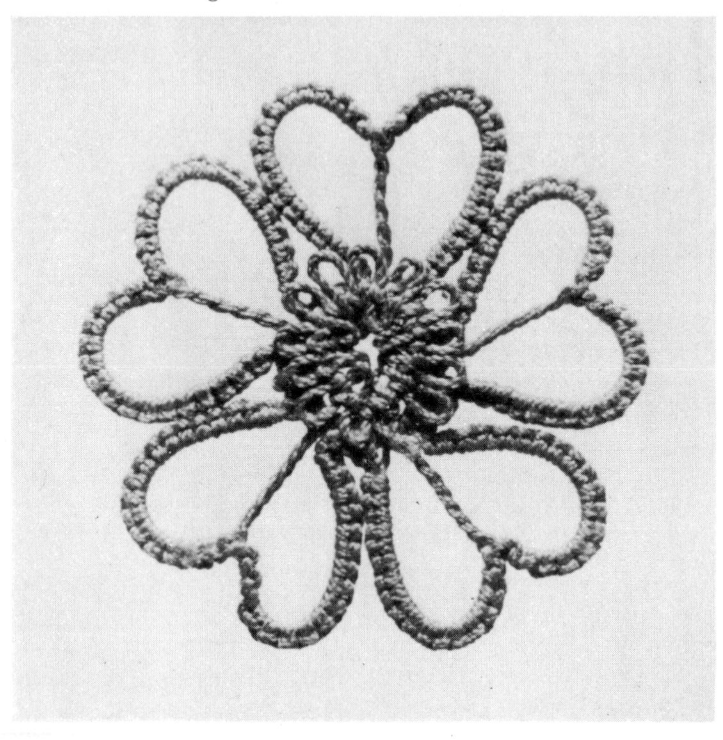

Fig. II 27

For elaboration, the petals may carry two additional long picots, one on either side of the twist, for fraying. The flower is then not quite so graceful, as the petals become wider at the base, but the 'filled' petals compensate for this.

The simulated picot—'climbing out' of a ring

This is an old method but so effective it could well be revived. If a ring is followed by a chain it is possible to 'climb out' from the ring after closure by way of its two threads, which form a false or simulated picot on leaving it. The chain, for which new threads are not required, starts from the new picot tip. This ingenious method can result in new and interesting formations, developed from the simple early form, which is as follows.

On a continuous thread make a ring, carrying one picot less than the number you finally want: in the model the number is five. Start with two doubles, work four measured picots two doubles apart, and end with two doubles.

Close the ring, turn it over and make a locking stitch, followed by 1 purl, at a distance from the ring equal in length to the other measured picots; you now have five.

Turn back again and work the surrounding chain for twelve doubles (or more), and join to the next picot, continuing round until you return to the start. The model shows the ring with the chain not quite completed: it will end by tying into the simulated picot.

This is a useful flower and quick to make. It can carry additional small picots between the long ones. Shown in Fig. II. 28.

One of the advantages of this method is that you can make a ring of *adjoining* picots equally spaced all round, and so correctly balanced, as the simulated picot dispenses with the inevitable and unwanted extra double normally required.

Fig. II 28

Decorative uses

A belt of stars (two working shuttles)

This consists of a row of rings or stars carried on the lower edge of the belt, enclosed by an upper chain. In the previous model you 'climbed out' of the ring. Here you not only climb out but you climb in as well, forming the ring between those two movements.

Start the foundation chain (on two shuttles) with five doubles. Work a ring on the second shuttle carrying three measured picots, 2ds apart starting and ending with 2ds (Total 8ds), at a distance away from the chain equal to the length of a drawn-up picot. (It is difficult to estimate this, as the thread stretches when the ring is drawn up).

On closure bring the thread down to the chain, but leaving the appropriate length to form the other side of the picot with which you started. Incorporate it into the chain, first shuttle in hand. You have now a four-pointed star arising from the lower chain, standing on a simulated picot.

Continue the chain for five doubles, counting the joining stitch and its purl, then make a second ring as first, but instead of the first picot, join into the picot of the preceding star. Repeat for the required length. The enclosing chain on the upper edge faces inwards, picking up the stars as it progresses. The model Fig. II 29 shows a ring whose final picot is waiting to be brought into the foundation chain for its completion.

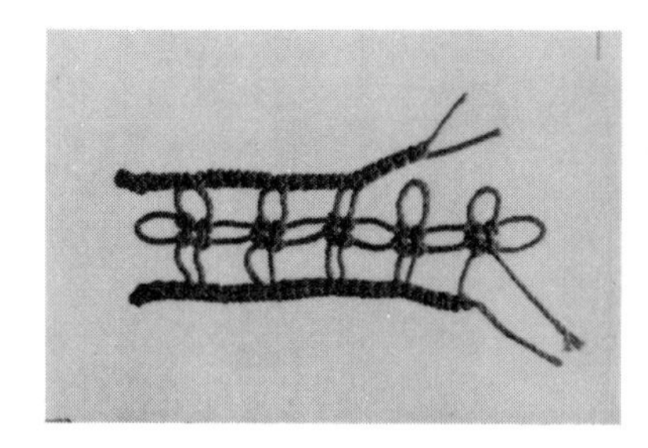

Fig. II 29

A medallion with a border of stars

A belt of stars can be modified to form a circle, which is more advanced work. The interior is intended to be simple: it can be made before or after the belt, according to choice. The foundation chain carrying the rings is in single pearl tatting. There are therefore three threads: two working shuttles on a continuous thread, the second making the rings: the third extra thread lies below them, making the pearls on the under side.

To work: start the chain with one double on the pair of shuttles. Take the third thread, leaving a few inches of 'tail', and work one double with it, facing down. The chain now consists of two doubles, one from each auxiliary.

On the second shuttle work the ring as in the previous model, on completion drawing the thread down into the chain. (These rings are set at an angle and do not join to one another but twice to the enclosing chains.) As the sequence of one up, one down, is never broken, the next stitch will be a lower pearl.

Now work three upper pearls, tight, the lower following automatically, upside down. After the last lower, join into the nearest picot on the ring with one double: a lower, and then immediately start the next ring. They are set as close together as possible when in a circle. Continue until you have made sixteen rings, ending with the upper double bringing in the last picot.

You now have to join start to finish, and you will have four threads to conceal, the fourth being the tail of the lower thread which ties into the last lower picot of the chain. Weave the four ends in and out of the back, making as near as possible an invisible join, the first and last rings very close together. A neat finish of pearl tatting is always difficult with so many thread ends.

If you have made the pearl chain first, which considering its rigidity is possibly the better way, the centre-piece will join into the appropriate lower pearl—the one under the junction of the two rings. If not, you must join to picots on the centre with this pearl as you come to it.

The centre piece consists of a central ring carrying four picots ten doubles apart. A chain is worked starting from one of the picots and forms an arch joining at midway to the pearl chain, fifteen doubles on either side. It returns to the central

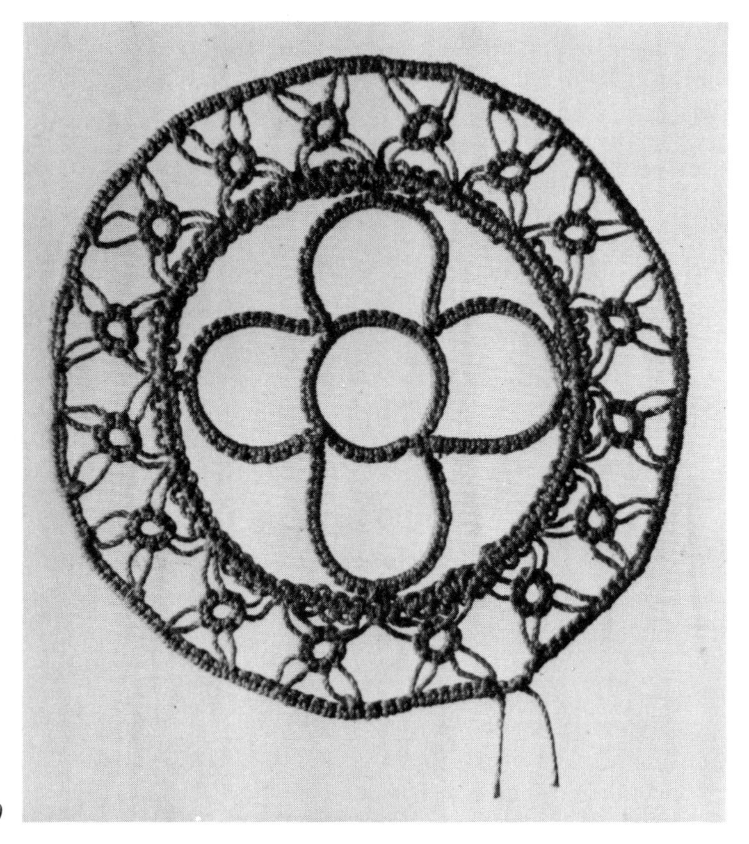

Fig. II 30

ring to which it joins with the shuttle thread, and repeats the arch three times. Several refinements can be used in the centre-piece, which, though not apparent, contribute towards its neatness. In the model the central ring is actually a mock ring, telescoped, although it is rather large for this, and is not beginners' work. On closure the chain climbs out through one of its picots, and continues to form the arches; thus the whole is worked on one pair of threads instead of two.

The outer round is a normal chain starting with a link-loop, the stitches facing in, to pick up the picots of the stars. Always start a circular chain between two joins—never at a picot which it would pull permanently out of line. There are six doubles between rings and twelve between the two picots on each ring. To get the tension correct and even on this round is difficult. As an alternative, make the outer round a pearl chain also: actually this is easier as it has no tension problems. Shown in Fig. II. 30.

If you find the insertion of the centre-piece difficult, which it is, omit it and use the belt alone. It is effective on a lampshade where the stars show to advantage. In this case the outer round should also be pearl.

Fig. II 31

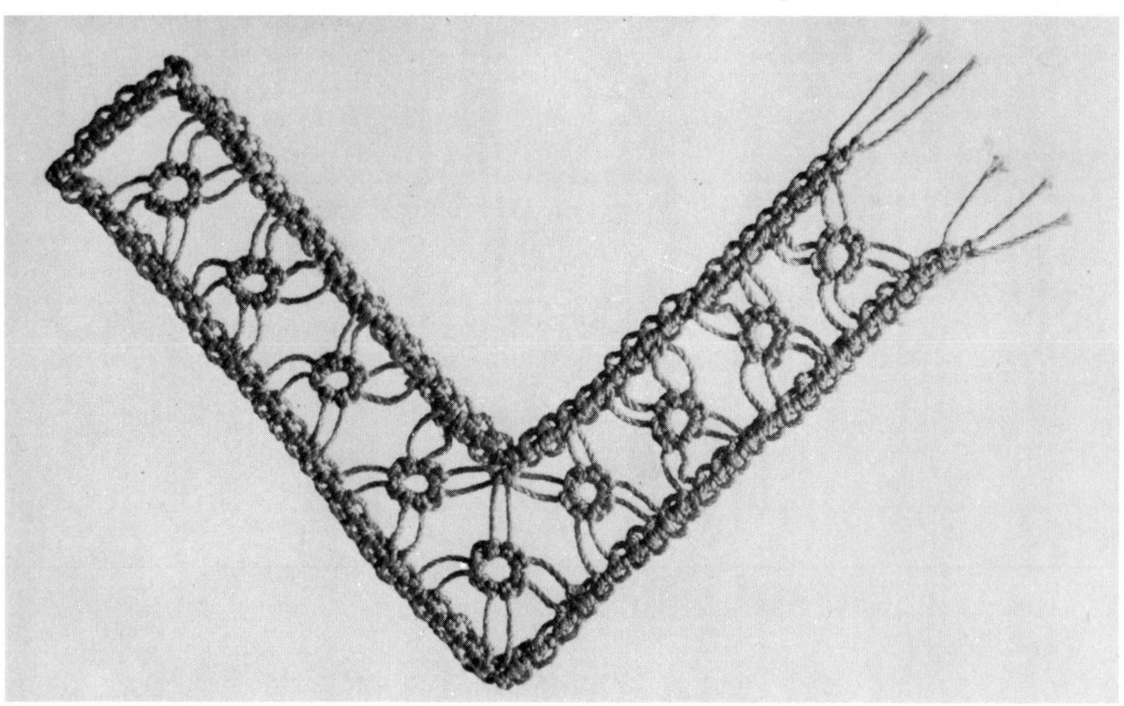

A right-angled strip

This formation of stars—using two pearl chains—can also turn a right angle, with which you can construct a square frame, or a Vandyke. A right-angle is shown in Fig. II. 31. Both upper and lower chains start at the top left side corner, outer edge.

Other arrangements are also possible. A number of adjoining picots, on a ring, mock ring or chain, can be massed closely together, to form circular or straight solid bands, an independent chain worked with a needle holding them together. As a stunt, Cupid's Bow, using massed graduated picots, is an illustration, whose only use would be to ornament a Valentine card.

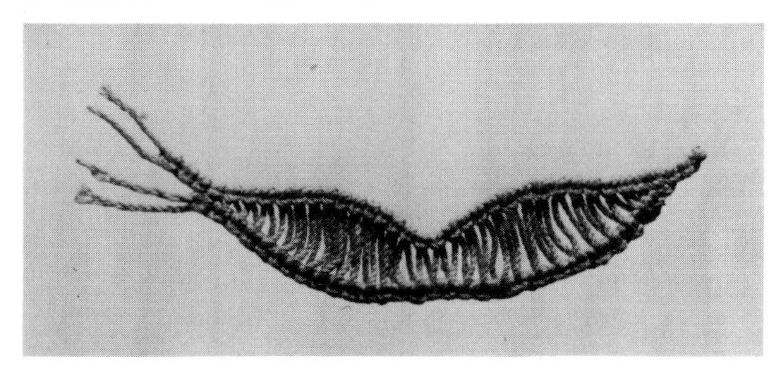

Fig. II 32

THE JOIN

The modern join was a long time evolving, and early pattern writers were forced to experiment with primitive methods of their own. Tatting had developed quite a long way before it was integrated into the work, for the earliest joins were made by hand. When all the separated pieces were completed they were sewn down in position on tissue paper, and picot was tied to picot, the ends cut off short. Later needle and thread were used to apply one row of rings upon another. This was an improvement, as the needle could pass through a picot and so make a real join, but a primitive one. For a short period the shuttle was abandoned altogether and the whole work done with a needle. Eventually the auxiliary thread (or rather the triangle round the hand making the ring) was drawn through a picot, as now: this was one of the two great tatting discoveries of the last century.

The join, by whatever method, is a nuisance to all pattern writers, complicating an otherwise simple formula. English patterns do treat it very seriously in that they announce when it occurs, and to what picot, but many foreign writers do not, often concluding their patterns with the statement 'for joins, consult the illustration', which may or may not be adequate. Those who evade giving the information use one of two methods. They do not mention a join, but record it as a picot instead, which you convert into a join where appropriate. This has advantages in that the pattern is simpler and shorter, and you have a choice as to where you will begin in a complicated piece of different groupings. Conversely they may, in a simple circle of joined rings, state a join in all of them, although there is nothing for the first ring to join to. Therefore you make a picot instead. This dispenses with a special starting ring. Both these methods are practical, though confusing when you meet them for the first time.

Mignonette stitch

In the foregoing sections you have learnt different types of joins: there is still another whose situation in a pattern, rather than the join itself, gave it its distinctive title. It is not a special stitch, but its description fits in best here. 'An arrangement of one or more rings joined to a single thread upon which they are free to move.' It is an old form (Riego's) not much seen now—the name has died out—but very attractive for mats.

When you join into a small picot in the normal way, the join holds the ring or chain in place because there is not room to move: the picot is only large enough to take the joining thread. If the picot is large, it can move along it, treating it as a running line. In a medallion formed round a centre picot this is exactly what happens: the joins are free to move right or left until the last one is in. The join is to a picot, but it could equally well be described as a join to a *thread.* The thread in fact need not be a picot at all, but a space of considerable length. Small rings can join at half-way in their construction to such spaces, whether arranged in a circle or rectangle. This is mignonette stitch.

A mignonette mat consists entirely of this formation, apart from its central ring. Each successive round consists of longer measured spaces, into each of which a small ring joins. The whole is stiffly (spray) starched, after pinning it out on a board at high tension. Details of work are not given, but a mat is shown in Fig. II. 33.

Fig. II 33

LETTERING

Lettering is a highly specialised art, for which a knowledge of styles, proportion and spacing is essential. Letters in tatting are possible in a few limited styles, but however good the tatting may be, unless the lettering itself is good, it is best left alone.

The only record I can find of its use is that made by Queen Marie, who applied it to ornamentation in the Greek Church, and some secular pieces, usually as large capitals. Large ornamented letters, say six inches in height, can hold their shape, if solidly constructed. As such they can be used in modern church work, and on banners. Fig. II. 34, the Royal Cypher, is an example of plain lettering in ordinary tatting, built up of curves. The E is easy, the R is not, requiring interplay of two shuttles.

Perhaps the most practical application is in very small simple letters worked in plain tatting or in node stitch, which can form a signature for a mounted piece, or be applied to a handkerchief.

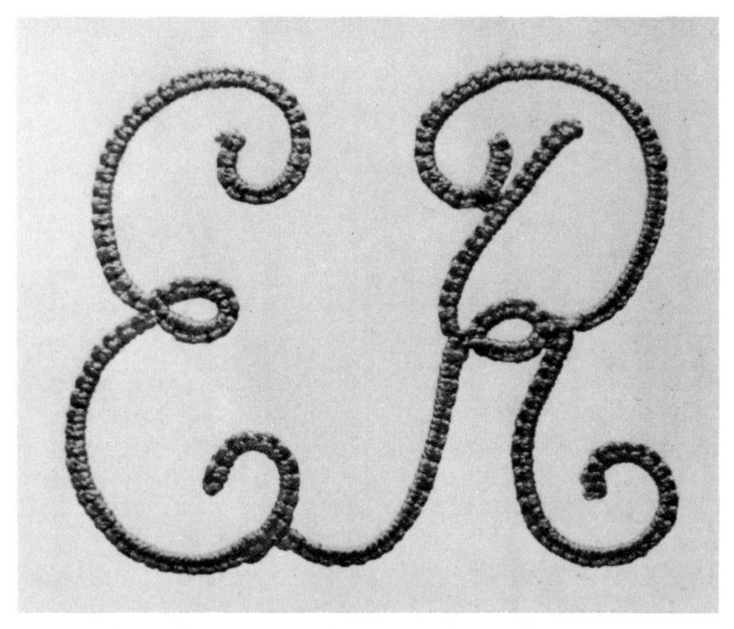

Fig. II 34

ADDITIONAL ORNAMENT: JEWELS AND BEADS

This subject is fully dealt with in Irene Waller's book, *Tatting*, and only very simple examples are given here, to show how a few beads (in this case pearls) can emphasise the lines of the design when worked into the fabric, not sewn on afterwards. Beads may be strung on the ball thread, shuttle thread or both. If on the ball, when at the appropriate point in the chain (worked with stitches facing down), the bead is slipped into position and the chain continued. The star-shaped piece (Fig. II. 35) is made in this manner, a second bead following the first, one double between them. In the small ring carrying four beads (Fig. II. 36), they are on the shuttle thread: if working with a needle they can be picked up one at a time, as required, which is easier than winding them on the shuttle. The little pendant (Fig. II. 37) is a mock-ring carrying three 'triplets': the beads are on both threads, which is more difficult. The first and third beads are on the running thread: the middle lower one is on the ball. After slipping up the first bead, work 1 plain: then place a bead from the ball next to it, and work 1 purl. Then place the third bead and continue with a normal chain. The position of the middle bead forces the other two inwards. Note that to string the beads you must have a needle which will take the thread, and be thin enough to pass through the bead.

Fig. II 35

Fig. II 36

Fig. II 37

Fig. II 38

The other two examples are in node stitch (Fig. II. 38) and single-pearl tatting (Fig. II. 39) respectively. In node stitch the beads are on the ball, and appear right and left automatically. In the single-pearl band, the beads are on the two auxiliaries. This is the most suitable of the five models for a first attempt. To keep the band straight, work the upper line in the sequence 1 pl, 1 pu (a normal double) and the lower in reverse, i.e. 1 pu, 1 pl.

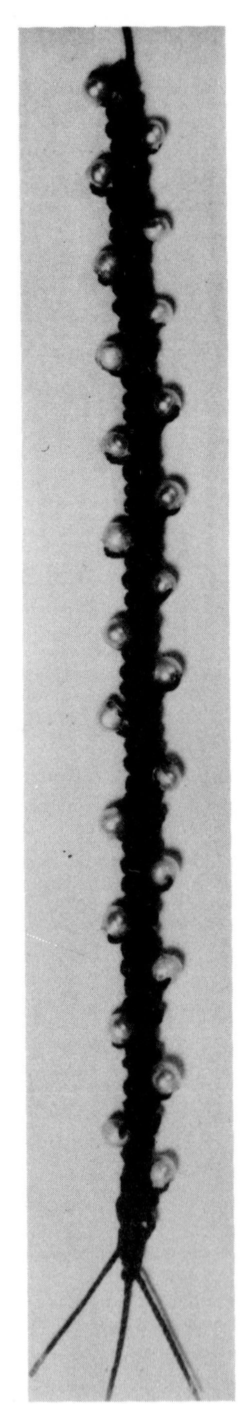

Fig. II 39

SOME COMPLETED WORK

A number of the special features described above appear in the plates of completed work.

PLATE I shows a plaque made for the Greek Church, consisting of four Greek letters made in single pearl, mounted on gold-coloured silk. Two of them are outlined in white 'run-out' stitch.

Thistles and Corn, in PLATE II, are an example of flower work. My book, *A New Look in Tatting*, gives a number of flowers and leaves including the wild rose, sprays of honeysuckle, blackberries, thistles and blades of corn. The patterns for these last two have been revised and the results are shown here. Long picots, cut and frayed, form the crown of the thistle. The body consists of curved chains (new) passing over and under but unjoined. Node stitch is employed for the outline and the stem, but this is optional. If ordinary chains are used, the 'pulled-over' picot technique is necessary. The chains are worked normally, facing out, with picots to which the crossing chains join. The picots are pulled forward from underneath so that they face inwards to receive them, where they are ended off. On reaching the base, the threads from the chains of both sides unite to form the stalk. In the blades of corn, each ear is a half ring, the unworked space of thread covered with stitches carried on the following ring.

Threads of different calibre can be used in the same picture, which gives a more realistic effect. Since flower work involves threads of many carefully graded colours, home dyeing will probably be necessary. To assemble flowers on a mount is a form of drawing and painting, and is as much an expression of the worker's skill as is their construction.

Rose Flamboyant, PLATE III, is an advanced piece. The outside edge is in ordinary tatting in multiple threads of cotton No. 10. Also in No. 10 is the outline of the design, but in node stitch, single threads. The seven flames are in sewing silk. They are composed of rings (about five to a flame) carrying long graduated picots, which are picked up by a normal chain in lead-coloured Sylko. The rings are not joined to one another, but lie on an adhesive background.

PLATE V consists of two hearts in cotton No. 60. They show graduated, massed and twisted picots, frayed threads, flower forms, over and under joins, scallops and 'medallion centre' with rings on a second shuttle.

PLATE VI, entitled Frivolité, is entirely in node stitch. The piece on the left, Climbing Plant, shows all the features described in the forthcoming sections. Five interlocking mock-rings show over and under joins: they do not actually join to one another, but are tied together by their thread ends. The five, differently arranged, could form the symbol of the Olympic Games. A spray of rose-leaves shows picots on both sides of the midrib, most of which stand free, to give a less rigid effect. A cube in perspective demonstrates acute and obtuse angles, and tassels of frayed threads.

None of these examples are beginners' pieces. They have been selected to show some of the variations of which node stitch is capable.

CONCLUSION

It is hoped that the special stitch arrangements, old and new, described in Part II, will help to enlarge the experience of every worker. The list can never be complete, for everyone can add to it something original of their own.

Tatting is a craft that is sustained entirely by voluntary workers, for that is what we all are. It earns nobody's living: it is practised simply for the pleasure it gives. We owe such pleasure to the vision, skill and ingenuity of the early pioneers to whom honour is due, but they designed so that others might follow. If no one did, their work would perish. You can help to keep it alive, encouraged perhaps by some of the suggestions offered. The future of the work lies entirely in our hands. Our voluntary contributions are essential for its very continuance, for it is only through them that the craft can survive.

Plate V

Plate VI

Part III

NODE STITCH

DEFINITION

Node stitch, which is original, was first published in 1962, before it was fully developed. Since then its behaviour has been explored and brought under control through the application of the rules here suggested. Their practice will give you command of a stitch form whose properties will allow effects that are beyond the scope of ordinary tatting.

Node stitch forms a line which stands slightly higher than the normal, carrying small nodes on either side alternately, which are visible when viewed from above. Tilted over half-way—to you or from you—the nodes are visible on one side only. In the normal chain the stitches are all facing upwards, causing a natural curve to the piece. In node stitch they face both ways—the two edges are the same—and the curve is lost. The chain, straight as worked, can be curved in either direction, one of its main attributes. The under surface presents a pronounced zig-zag, which is useful for special effects. On account of this, both rings and chains are always worked on the upper surface, for they cannot be worked on the reverse side.

Brief references to node stitch have been made from time to time in Part II. In the section on the Stitch, its development from the two twists is explained, resulting in the formation of nodes. To obtain these, the normal sequence of the two half-stitches is disrupted, and replaced by two consecutive stitches of one kind, followed by two of the other, thus making four stitches to a sequence, instead of two.

GENERAL PROPERTIES OF NODE STITCH

Node stitch can do what normal chains can do, and rather more. It can perform the following functions, described as 'features'.

1. Raise a picot on the upper edge, and join to an existing one within reach.
2. Drop a picot on the lower edge, and join to an existing one within reach.
3. Carry a ring on a second shuttle, on the upper edge.

A ring on the lower edge is not possible unless you can use your left hand to make it, since the stitch cannot be worked on the reverse side, but there are ways of overcoming this. The directions which follow show how to express the features in a pattern, and how to work them. A demonstration chain is illustrated and described, incorporating all the features, upper and lower.

Plate VII

The three forms of tatting: right, ordinary tatting; below left, pearl tatting; below right, node stitch.

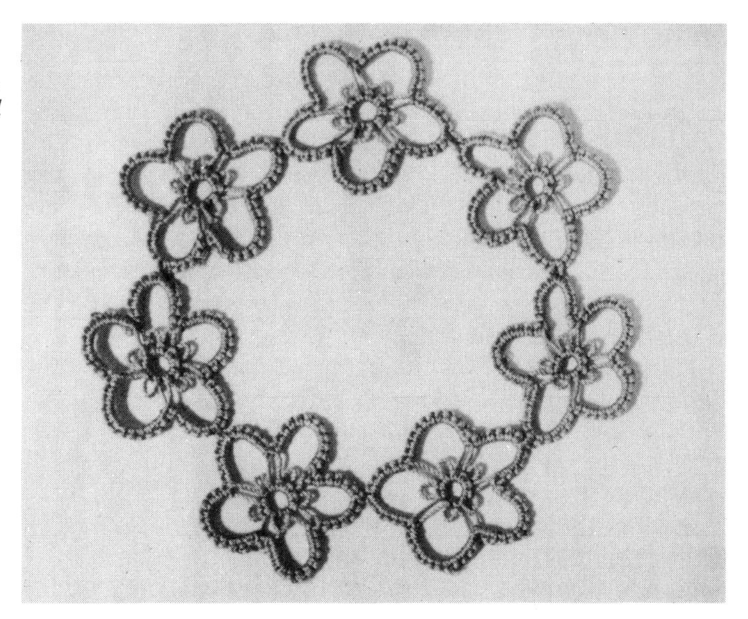

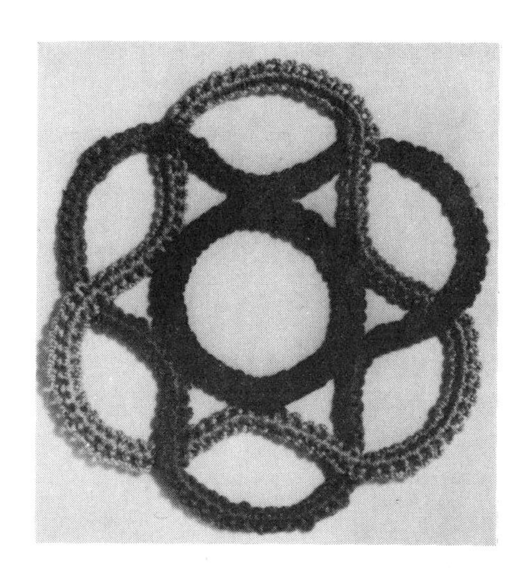

PRELIMINARY PRACTICE

In node stitch the shuttle thread lies on the *top* of the chain instead of nearest to you, from which point it forms nodes alternating on either side, working in correct sequence. Two similar stitches (of either kind) will bring the thread into this position, described as 'neutral'. From then on nodes will form automatically; 2 pu make a node on the upper edge, 2 pl on the lower, the node preceding the stitches which make it. This pair of nodes is one sequence: once started, the sequence is *never broken* throughout the chain.

The actual start of a chain is rather complicated, but for simply practising the making of nodes you can work a chain by knotting the shuttle and ball threads together, going straight into the sequence with 2 pl, 2 pu, or 2 pu, 2 pl, as you choose. As you are starting hard up against a knot, hold it so that the shuttle thread lies above the ball, i.e. in neutral. Without a knot (as in a ring) the first couple could not produce a node: with the knot, it can. Continue with the sequence until you have mastered the rhythm, making the nodes neat and tight, just visible when viewed from above. Keep this piece for further development.

You have now made a section of chain, which is simple, but you cannot as yet do precise work, let alone record and repeat it, without some framework of established technique. This needs further knowledge and it is hoped that you will think it worthwhile to acquire in order to obtain full mastery over the stitch, as so much can be accomplished with it.

RECORDING THE PATTERN

In ordinary tatting the double stitch is the unit and the number used to make a ring or chain is recorded. In node stitch the nodes are the units, not the stitches, and moreover since nodes appear on both sides of the line, either one can be selected by the pattern writer. Whichever side you use must be mentioned at the start of the formula. If you count on the upper edge you are using Upper Count—UC. If the lower, the initials LC signify this. This does not apply to rings which are always on the upper (or outside) count.

CHOICE OF COUNT

The count you choose depends on the advantage one will give over the other in the particular chain—or section of chain—you are working. Normally either is suitable, and the whole piece can be done on either count. There are situations, however, where a particular one is more convenient. At present you cannot visualise these, but the most obvious is the shape of the chain. The one which places the countable nodes on the convex side of the curve so that they are more clearly seen, is preferable. If the chain makes S-bends curving in two directions, the count may be changed at a join without disturbing the sequence. In Stylised Flower Spray there are long chains with double curves, but it has not been always possible to arrange for all the counted nodes to be on the convex side, as no join was available.

Mirror image chains, where one is the reflection of the other, often occur. By using upper and lower count respectively you not only count on the convex side, but both chains start from the same relative point (for example the centre) instead of one working outwards and the other inwards, giving easier adjustment of tension and ensuring correct balance of the piece.

Therefore it is important to be familiar with handling both counts from the beginning. One is no more difficult than the other, and by selecting the most suitable both the pattern and the work can be simplified.

THE FORMULA

Figures standing alone in the formula represent the number of nodes showing on the countable edge, between features. Nodes on the opposite side are not indicated, for as the sequence is never broken, these follow automatically. (You cannot make two consecutive nodes of one kind.) *They are understood and not recorded*, for the formula is only concerned with nodes on the selected side.

Picots and joins, however, which are features breaking up the chain into sections, must be indicated on whichever side they occur, irrespective of the type of count, upper or lower.

A section of chain (where the thread is already in neutral) consisting of five nodes on upper count would be written simply as 5. Stop when the fifth node is made. Do not continue with two plain in an attempt to round off the sequence—'5 upper nodes' means just this and nothing more. This does not contradict the statement above, i.e. that a lower node follows automatically, which applies to a chain which is going to continue. Here the fifth upper node is at the end of a line—nothing else follows. You will have worked four and a half sequences.

The formula is sufficient to describe a piece, but it can be supplemented by a diagram which shows every stitch, above and below. This of course takes up more space, but it is easier to work from as it does give a complete picture of the work.

THE DIAGRAM

Whether for chain or ring, a horizontal line represents the running thread upon which the stitches lie. Two small vertical strokes above it represent two purl stitches, or an upper node: below it they indicate two plain. If more than one pair of nodes is present, the total can be bracketed together in the usual way. Fig. III. 1a shows the formula and diagram for five upper nodes. In the diagram the two purl outside the bracket constitute the fifth.

(UC) 5

4 (II II) II

Fig. III 1a

THE PICOT AND THE JOIN

Both these occur in their correct place in the sequence. Picots are developed nodes, i.e. by leaving a space between the two couples a picot is formed in the usual way. It has not replaced a node, which is still there, but enlarged, to become a feature. Two purl causes a raised or upper picot, two plain a dropped one. The node count begins again after the picot. The production of picots on both sides of the chain is one of the great advantages of the work. For practice revive your original node stitch chain and form picots, first all on one side, then all on the other and finally on both sides, alternating, spacing them as you choose: you do not have to use every node.

In the formula it is shown as P, which includes the two stitches which make it. An arrow follows the P, indicating whether it is above or below. In the diagram the two stitches are represented by a special picot sign, which is two produced or developed stitch strokes. This is logical because the picot is a developed node. An arrow is not necessary because the picot sign is placed either above or below the line.

The stitches involved in a Join are in a position otherwise occupied by a node, which they replace. To effect an upper join, work as follows. Instead of starting an upper node, when due, draw the auxiliary through the picot, pick up the thread with the shuttle in the normal way and draw both threads very tightly so that the join is hard up against the chain. This is the joining stitch. Follow closely with one purl, and continue the sequence.

To make the join on the lower edge, work in the same way, but in the position of a lower node, and follow the joining stitch with one plain.

In the formula J represents the joining stitch, followed by an arrow to give its position. The appropriate single stitch is not recorded, as the arrow tells you which it is (purl up, plain down). In the diagram, which also uses J, the single is shown, as here every stitch is accounted for. The pair occupy the space of one node.

To demonstrate the method of recording these two features the formulae and diagrams are given of examples of each.

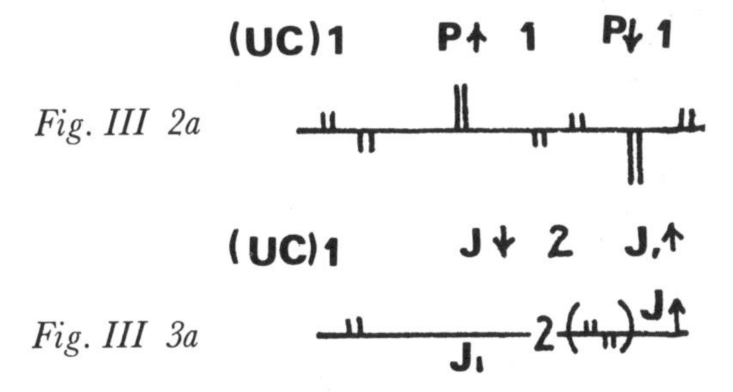

Fig. III 2a

Fig. III 3a

The first consists of a node, an upper picot, a node, a lower picot, and ends with one node. The second shows a lower and an upper join separated by two nodes. The positions of picots and joins in the two examples are intentionally different, but their respective lengths are the same, as they carry the same number of stitches (seven couples). The formulae have been spaced out to fit their respective diagrams, so that you can see the relationship between the two. (Figs. III. 2a and III. 3a.)

Practise these with a piece of string, thin and supple, working it with the fingers. The nodes will be large and bold, and the sequence much easier to see. Make a short strip carrying a few spaced picots, then another strip, joining to them. Start the chains with a knot, as you did in the preliminary practice piece.

The foregoing examples represent a *part* of any existing chain—the start is not included, but it must now be considered. There are four methods of starting, and each can be adjusted for upper or lower count, but they are not as formidable as they appear. Two stitches are involved in all the starts, before the sequence begins. The first is dictated by the nature of the start, the second prepares for the count you have selected.

THE CHAIN START: (CHST)

The stitch involved in the start itself depends on the position of the chain in the pattern. It may follow a ring (No. 1), start from a picot (No. 2), start spontaneously with a blind end (No. 3) or a link-loop (No. 4). In patterns, the starts are referred to by number. The second stitch, which follows, is either a single plain, or a purl.

SETTING THE COUNT

Since you are counting nodes, it is important that the first one is clearly seen, upper or lower as the case may be. To make it more obvious the first node of the chain should be well clear of the start. Therefore you make one single stitch of the opposite kind, thus placing it slightly away. For upper count the first node should lie on the upper edge. Therefore your 'single' stitch is a plain which does not produce a node by itself. Then go into the sequence with 2 pu, 2 pl. For lower count it is a purl, which will bring the first node to the lower edge, when followed by the sequence 2 pl, 2 pu. On making this single stitch, keep the shuttle thread well up to get it into neutral. This refinement may seem unnecessary, but it allows you to see more easily which count you are on, of importance when you are copying a piece without a pattern.

ADDITIONAL SYMBOLS

A single plain stitch is represented by a short stroke below the line. For a purl stitch it lies above it. For an unturned purl a small u is attached to the stroke. (Upu in the formula.) A loop (Lo) at the head of a line containing an arrow indicates that it will be telescoped in. Without the arrow it will remain there.

DETAILS OF THE FOUR STARTS

ChSt 1 is a slight exception. Following a ring, the threads are already there, but there is no previous starting stitch.

Therefore you make two singles of the same kind, 2 pl for upper count, 2 pu for lower. In this position they cannot make a node, and are not part of the sequence, therefore they are shown as two stitches. They have brought the thread into neutral, and the sequence now begins. This start is not much used, and need not be practised. Examples of the four starts, all on upper count, follow. They all consist of two and one half sequences.

Fig. III 4a **(UC) 2 pl 3**

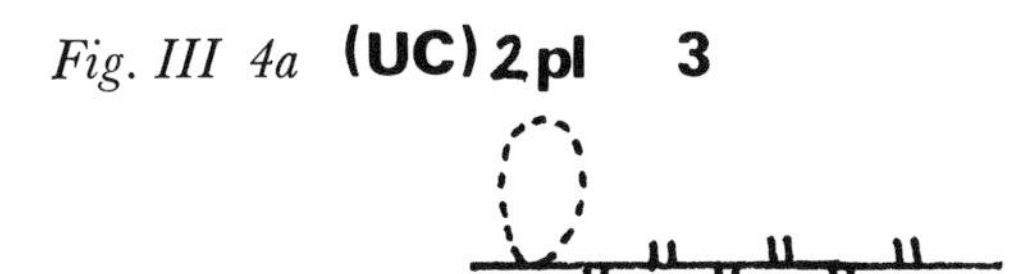

ChSt 1

Here the chain follows a ring, as in a scroll. For upper count work 2 pl, then go into the sequence with 2 pu, 2 pl. For lower count, work 2 pu: sequence 2 pl, 2 pu.

Fig. III 5a **(UC) J←1pl 3**

ChSt 2

From a picot. Join the auxiliary into the picot in the normal way, and holding the shuttle thread above (in neutral), work the appropriate single for the count required. Follow with the sequence.

Fig. III 6a **(UC) Lo 1pu 1pl 3**

ChSt 3

With a blind end. Make a loop with a single purl, work the appropriate single and start the sequence, telescoping the loop in.

Fig. III 7a **(UC) Lo Upu 1pl 3**

ChSt 4

With a link-loop at the head. Make as No. 3 but do not turn the purl, thus locking it.

Note that for these two starts, the stitch making the loop is always a purl, irrespective of what follows. A plain may cause the loop to twist over.

Practise these starts, both upper and lower count, in thin string, which must be firm but supple. They are simpler than they appear, quick to make, and demonstrate clearly the position of the nodes.

THE DEMONSTRATION CHAIN

Both raised and dropped picots and joins are displayed. Their individual construction you have learnt and their recording. Here all the features are presented on one running line, with an unbroken sequence of nodes. The chain, which starts with a blind end, is divided into sections between each feature. The node count starts afresh from each feature and ends at the next one, whether above or below. This particular chain is deceptively simple. The distance between each is equal, consisting of four nodes, on both sides. To get this result, the features *must* alternate above and below, for they can only occur in their turn in the sequence. If they were all up, or all down, the sections would be equal, but if one or more is carried on the opposite side one extra node would appear, and the section would be that much longer: therefore the features would not be equidistant. There are altogether sixteen possible permutations of the four. To understand the behaviour of a feature-bearing chain is not important at the moment, but it becomes necessary when you are designing for yourself. The chain, worked in string, is shown below, with its formula and diagram. You should be able to work it from either one. Shown in Figs. III. 8 and 8a.

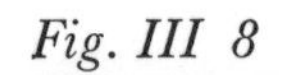

Fig. III 8

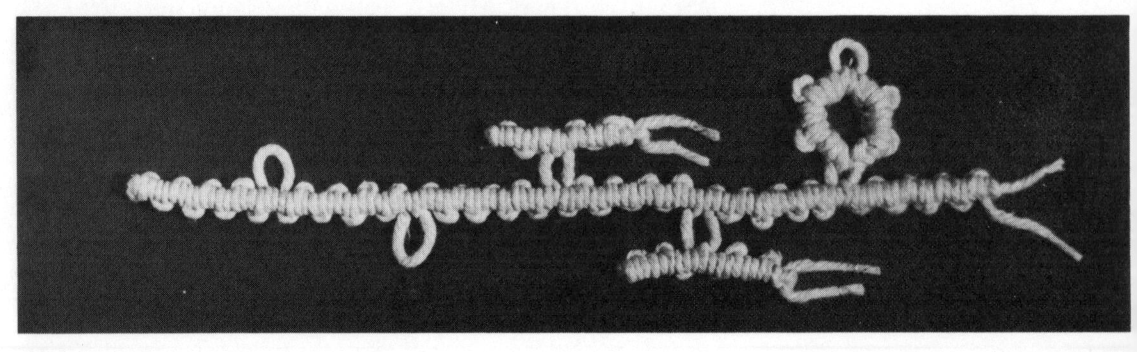

(UC) Lo lpu lpl 4 P↑ 4 P↓ 4 J↑ 4 J↓ 4 R2 pu 4

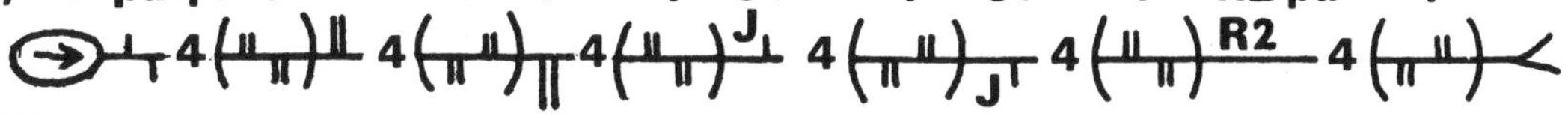

Fig. III 8a

The ring on the second shuttle

This last feature is a ring whose construction you have not yet learnt, but it is introduced to show that a chain in node stitch can make use of a second shuttle, as any other chain may. It is not of immediate importance, but since it constitutes one of the properties of the stitch, and the thread after making the ring has to be integrated back into the chain, it is shown here for future reference.

To include the ring, which might be called 'a second shuttle diversion', work as follows: after the two plain of a sequence on the chain, work the ring as near as possible to it. When drawn up bring the thread close in, and with the first shuttle make two purl stitches with it. Continue the sequence with two plain.

The two stalk threads which support the ring are not stitches, so they are disregarded. An upper node is due and the two purl perform this duty, although they do not apparently do so owing to the angle at which the second shuttle thread lies: a visible node does not form. The ring appears to be replacing an upper node but actually it does not. The ring on its stalks is therefore an 'extrusion', sandwiched in and preceding the two purl, which maintain the sequence. Nodes must be seen if they are to be counted.

Carried on a chain the ring with the following two purl would appear in a formula R: 2 pu. In the diagram, if the two purl are shown in the normal way—two strokes—they would look like a node which is not actually formed. We therefore must resort to the same description as that in the formula, R: 2, but omitting the pu as stitches above the line are inevitably purl.

THE RING IN NODE STITCH

The stitches on a ring are very closely packed together and tend to strangle the running thread. For this reason large rings are not possible. Small ones, however, are capable of some surprising effects, useful if used sparingly. Node stitch is really more suitable for all-chain designs, the small rings being regarded as ornament instead of a major part of construction.

When you draw a line of ordinary tatting into a circle the piece lies flat, as the thread carrying the stitches is in the interior, the stitches being all on one side of it, facing out. In node stitch the thread is on the top of the line above the zig-zag (the stitches). If loosely drawn up it can remain there and the inner nodes will just show, but if tight they will roll inwards, the thread taking the shortest course. In so doing, it displaces the stitches, tilting them out of their natural position. Really tight, with the running thread right inside the ring, the zig-zag takes up a position on the outer edge, with the result that the inner nodes vanish completely—the ring is actually resting on them, and the outer ones have moved upwards—picots produced from them would stand up vertically. The ring in fact has the same appearance on both surfaces, upper and lower.

Make two rings, each containing at least twelve sequences, and draw them up tight and slack respectively. Their very different appearance, including their size, is due entirely to tension.

The slack ring is the least attractive, being rather plain, its upper surface presenting a line of apparent 'overcast' stitches. The tight one has more character, as the overcast effect has rolled to the inside, and the serrated edge is prominent.

Manipulation of the ring

You can manipulate the slack ring to look like the tight one by simply turning it half inside-out, so that the zig-zag lies on the edge. This has a more relaxed effect than the very tight one, and is probably the best method, but you need practice for this if you want to make two rings of exactly the same size. The regulation of tension is an individual performance and cannot be measured. 'As tight as possible' is fairly definite, but 'slack' is not, and the result varies with the worker's interpretation. The five interlocking rings in Plate V were 'as tight as possible' (each of 24 sequences) for this reason.

When describing the properties of node stitch, it was stated that you could not make a ring on the second shuttle on the lower edge of a chain, unless you were left-handed, thus preventing crossing of threads with the ring worked right side up. Since you can make the ring appear the same on both surfaces, you can work either a slack one—manipulated—or one very tight, and simply pull it over to the lower edge, upside down. In this case make the ring when a lower node is due, and integrate the thread back into the chain with two plain. You cannot of course do this if joins are concerned.

Nodes and picots

Rings can start with either two plain or two purl (ending with the opposite) according to where you wish to place the nodes. The first half of the sequence will not of course produce a node, and you 'lose' it either outside or inside, whichever you need. As an example, the ring on the demonstration chain started with two purl. By so doing the first and last outer nodes stand well clear of the base, and show up clearly for the ornament which they are.

With a normally tight auxiliary, i.e. tightly made nodes, they will not be very obvious, even those in the interior of the slack ring, for however slack it is, they will still tend to roll under. As interior nodes are one of the special features of the node stitch ring, they should be encouraged to appear if the design needs them. To do this make them as link-picots. They will then stand out well. The interior nodes (especially in a small ring) are very close together. The effect is often better if you produce them alternately with tight nodes.

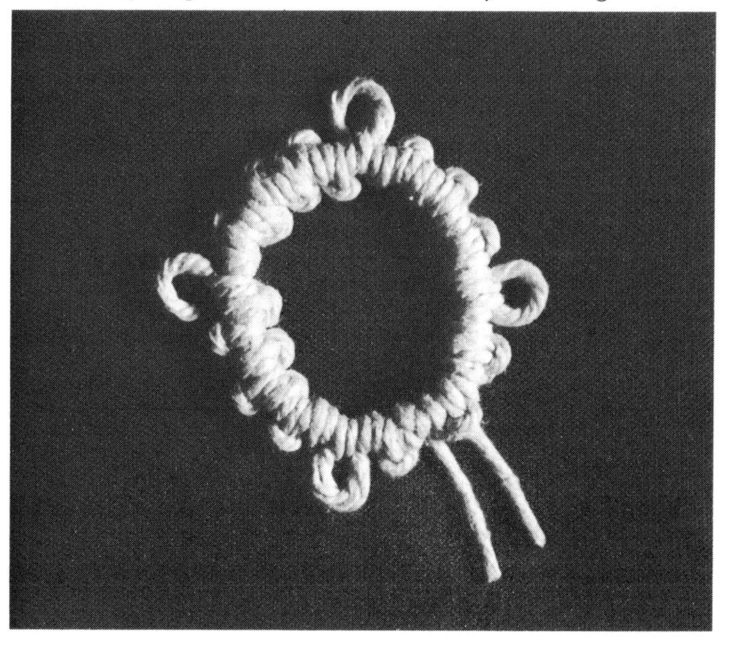

Fig. III 9

Upside down with all the nodes both outside and in as larger picots, the ring makes a good centre-piece for a flower.

Fig. III. 10 shows three rings. In the first, of twelve sequences, all the nodes are developed into link-picots. In the second, also of twelve, all are distinctly longer. It is shown on the reverse side.

The third is tight, with sixteen sequences, the outer nodes normal but well tilted up, and four equally spaced internal large picots. All the interior nodes have rolled out of sight. It starts with two purl: the following two plain produces the lower internal picot. Four outer nodes follow before the next picot in the interior. It needs care and adjustment on pulling up.

Position of rings in a design

Rings can follow one another, alternate with chains or be carried on one. In all these positions the two threads supporting them may legitimately show. In a ring however which is centrally placed, bearing precisely spaced picots to be joined by surrounding work, the threads entering and leaving should be as unobtrusive as possible. It should appear as an uninterrupted circle with no apparent beginning or ending. These two objectives cannot be obtained so successfully with a real ring. Therefore you make a mock-ring, and if not too large, preferably with a telescoping loop which occupies no space.

A real ring, carrying four equally spaced outer picots, three nodes between each, would be written simply as

Fig. III 10

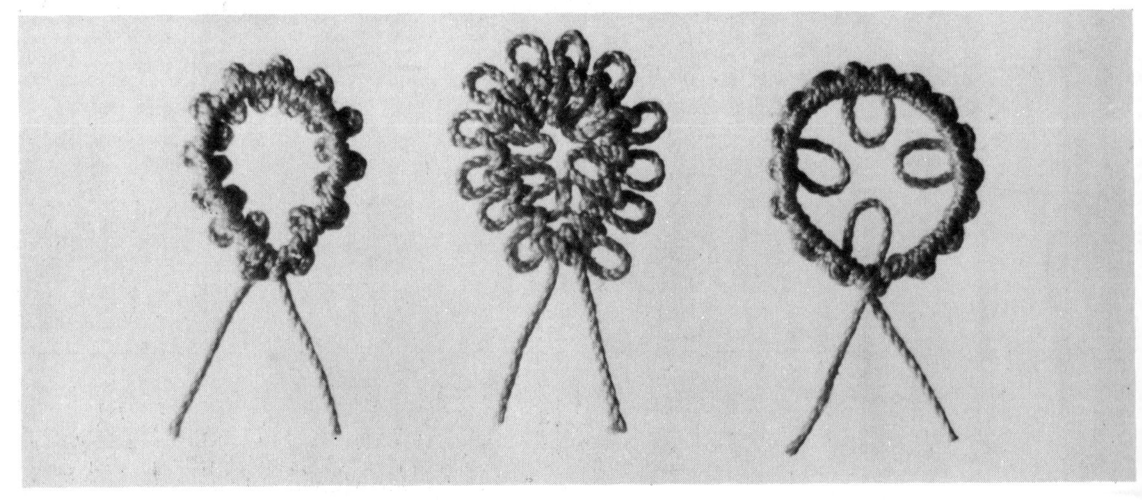

R: 4(3 P↑) which gives an overall impression of its formation. The start, which can be anywhere, is purposely left out. Its position is left to you, but a convenient point is prior to one node before a picot. The model, which is worked in string, is a mock-ring. Although you are making a chain, you are composing a circle, and the standard start needs a slight adjustment. The loop itself is made with two plain, which is also the start of the sequence. The first node is therefore 'lost' on the inside, which will not be noticeable. It is the outside edge which matters.

A PRACTICE PIECE

This is one long chain starting with a link-loop to which the end can eventually join. It carries long measured picots grouped in pairs: between a pair a small picot lies on the lower edge. All the distances between picots and pairs are optional, and the length of the picots: here the long ones are on Pin 6 on an eighth scale. It is no more than a practice piece, offering simply a start, upper and lower picots, and joins.

The formula is as follows: (UC) ChSt 4. 4 P↑ 1 P↓ 1 P↑.

From this you should be able to discern that after the start there are four upper nodes, then an upper picot: an upper node, the lower picot, an upper node and the second upper picot. This constitutes the repetition. Continue for as long as needed.

To make the curved end, work about twelve upper nodes (they will be inside the curve) then join to the nearest long picot and continue the repetition in reverse, substituting joins for picots.

Fig. III 11

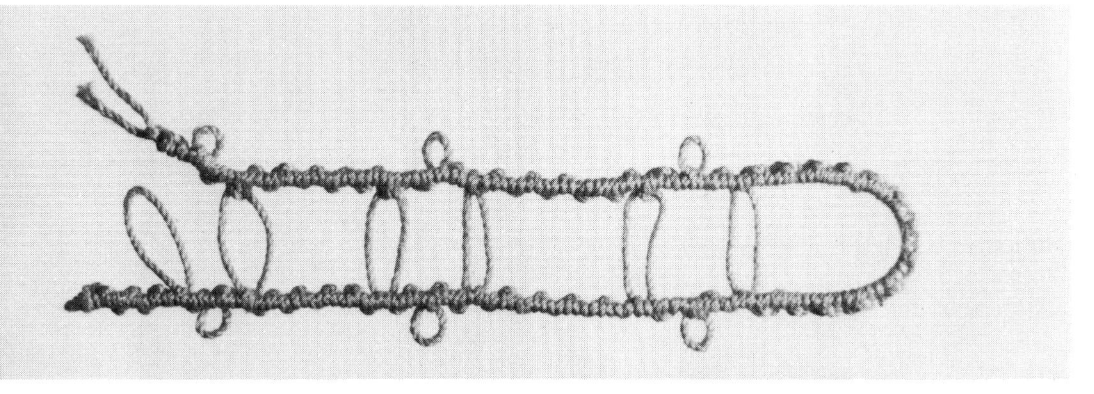

This piece could be equally well worked by starting with the upper line instead of the lower, and dropping the long picots instead of raising them. The example shows three pairs of long picots the last of which is waiting for the join. It is shown in the model Fig. III. 11. Work this piece before attempting the Flower Spray.

STYLISED FLOWER SPRAY *(See p. 116)*

There are easier flowers to work than this model, but it is chosen to demonstrate the use of the two counts, upper and lower. The three flower-heads, all differing slightly in design, are symmetrical pieces, one half being the mirror image of the other, for which the two counts are necessary.

A general description covering all three is as follows: One long chain curves to produce a flask-like form in the interior. To the flask another chain is attached on either side, described as accessory chains. The lengths of the flask chains and the accessories vary in the three models. An independently made ring carrying seven outer picots is placed, reverse side up, in the centre of the flask after mounting.

The central flower

In this the flask-chain is very long, as it provides, as well as the flask, the outside edges. The two accessories are very short. It starts with a link-loop, at the left side of the base of the flower. It travels upwards to form the outside edge, drops a picot for the accessory chain, curves round carrying three ornamental picots, makes a raised link-picot in the neck of the flask, continues down to form its left side, dropping a link-picot on the way, and when it reaches the base joins into its starting loop. The join is a lower one, so after the joining stitch work one plain, these two taking the place of a lower node.

Formula: (UC) ChSt 4. 12 Lp ↓ 6 3(P ↑) 1 Lp ↑ 4 Lp 7 J ↓ . You have now made the left outer edge and the left side of the flask. The base of the flask follows. Work an upper node and a link-picot facing down three times: 3(1 Lp). The first two links are for the stalk: the third eventually receives the end of the chain.

Now continue into the right side curve of the flask, which is a repeat of the left, in reverse: 7 Lp ↓ 4 J ↑ , 3(P ↑) 6 Lp ↓ 12. The join is to the link-picot in the neck of the flask.

On completion of the chain, cut threads, and tie temporarily into the nearest Lp at the base.

The accessory chains

These two chains are mirror images, and start from picots, therefore use ChSt 2, upper and lower count respectively, for right and left sides.

Right side: Join to the appropriate link-picot on the flask: work five upper nodes: cut threads.

Left side: Turn the work round (not over) and join to the picot on the left side of the flask. Work five lower nodes, and cut threads. Tie the ends from these chains temporarily into their respective picots: permanent connections will be made when the piece is mounted.

The stalk: the two link-picots at the base hold the stalk. On a new pair of threads draw the auxiliary through both picots making two long loops, and pass the shuttle through both loops simultaneously. Pull both threads very tightly and go straight into the sequence with a chain.

The upper flower

Here the chain forming the flask is much shorter. It does not make the outer edges, which are provided by long accessories, described as the right and left wings.

The flask chain starts with a link-loop high up on the shoulder of the flower, right side. By starting at this point the countable nodes will be on the convex side of the flask curves. After the start the chain carries four (upper) nodes, then a lower link-picot at the neck: four more nodes, and an upper link for the right wing. Again four nodes, then four upper links for the base.

The left side curve rises with four nodes, an upper link, four nodes, and a lower join to the picot at the neck. Finish the chain with four nodes, cut threads.

The right wing: (UC) ChSt 2 from the link on the right flank of the flask. Work 3 nodes, and two plain stitches. Make an upper join to the starting loop of the flask chain. Follow with two nodes and a locking stitch.

The descent to the base is eleven nodes. Make a lower join into the nearest link at the base, 2 pu stitches, and a single joining stitch into the next link. Cut threads, leaving a long shuttle thread which will be used as the auxiliary for the stalk.

The left wing: (lower count) (LC) ChSt 2 from the link on the left flank of the flask. Three nodes, a lower link-picot for the threads of the flask chain: two nodes and a locking stitch: descend to the base with eleven nodes.

Make an upper join into the nearest link-picot at the base, 2 pl stitches, and a single joining stitch into the next link. The threads from the two wings now meet. Cut off the auxiliary, leaving the shuttle thread intact: it is used for the stalk.

Fig. III 12

The stalk: Go straight into the chain, discarding the two old auxiliaries, which will be drawn through the mount.

The Lower Flower: this is the same construction as the upper, but in slightly different proportions, and details are not given.

Mounting: Adjust the tension of all the chains, undoing the temporary ties. The chains should be very tight. Instead of normal joins to the picots, the piece lies better if all ends are threaded on needles and simply passed through their respective picots and through the mount, taping them down at the back.

Mounting will take longer than the tatting and needs much patience. Press the pieces into shape, the flask well formed and lying dead centre. Sew down with the fewest stitches possible, in matching cotton. A stitch through the picot at the neck of the flask sets its position.

The central flower is the easiest, with its short accessory chains. Do not necessarily copy the arrangement of the model. The pieces are supplied for you to draw with, to form your own designs. The Spray is shown in Fig. III. 12.

THE SEQUENCE, VARIATIONS, AND ADJUSTMENT OF NODES

The sequence has throughout been described as 2.2. It is, however, quite possible to use 3.3 which gives a repetition of six stitches instead of four. As this is rather clumsy when concerned with the spacing of picots, reference to it has not been made. The point to make now is, a single stitch may be added to a node of two stitches, without disaster, and is scarcely apparent. Alternatively one may be subtracted to form a reduced node of one stitch only, although this is a momentary lapse into ordinary tatting. By this addition or subtraction you are lengthening or shortening a chain without interfering with the number of nodes it is intended to carry. This is applicable also in a circle centrally placed, where, for example, two interior picots must be directly opposite one another, as in Climbing Plant, where outside picots are also precisely spaced.

SOME FURTHER ATTRIBUTES OF NODE STITCH

With node stitch you can see exactly where you are in a pattern and the number of stitches you have worked, by simply counting the nodes. This is easier than counting double stitches in the ordinary way. It is especially useful when you want to produce a feature which ordinary tatting cannot do. It allows, for example, a picot to be dropped on an ordinary chain, sometimes of great convenience. Work the ordinary chain, and at the point required, after a normal double stitch work an extra purl, which will get the thread to the top of the work, i.e. in neutral. To make a dropped picot, continue with the ordinary double stitch. As you have followed the two purl with a plain, the picot will form on the under side. It is not necessary to work two plain: one is sufficient. The break will be scarcely noticeable.

CONCLUSION

It is hoped that this introduction to the stitch will arouse interest in its study. Workers to whom fine lace is the essence of tatting may feel that this is not their medium, for its inherent firmness does not make for suppleness. Delicacy however has been replaced by boldness of line, together with a certain liveliness, not without grace. It awaits further development by designers who can build on these attributes to produce forms of their own. The stitch is so adaptable that it applies equally well to geometrical, abstract and natural subjects. Its discovery brings as much liberation to tatting as the discovery of the chain, over one hundred years ago. It asks for fresh minds to explore the many directions it may take.

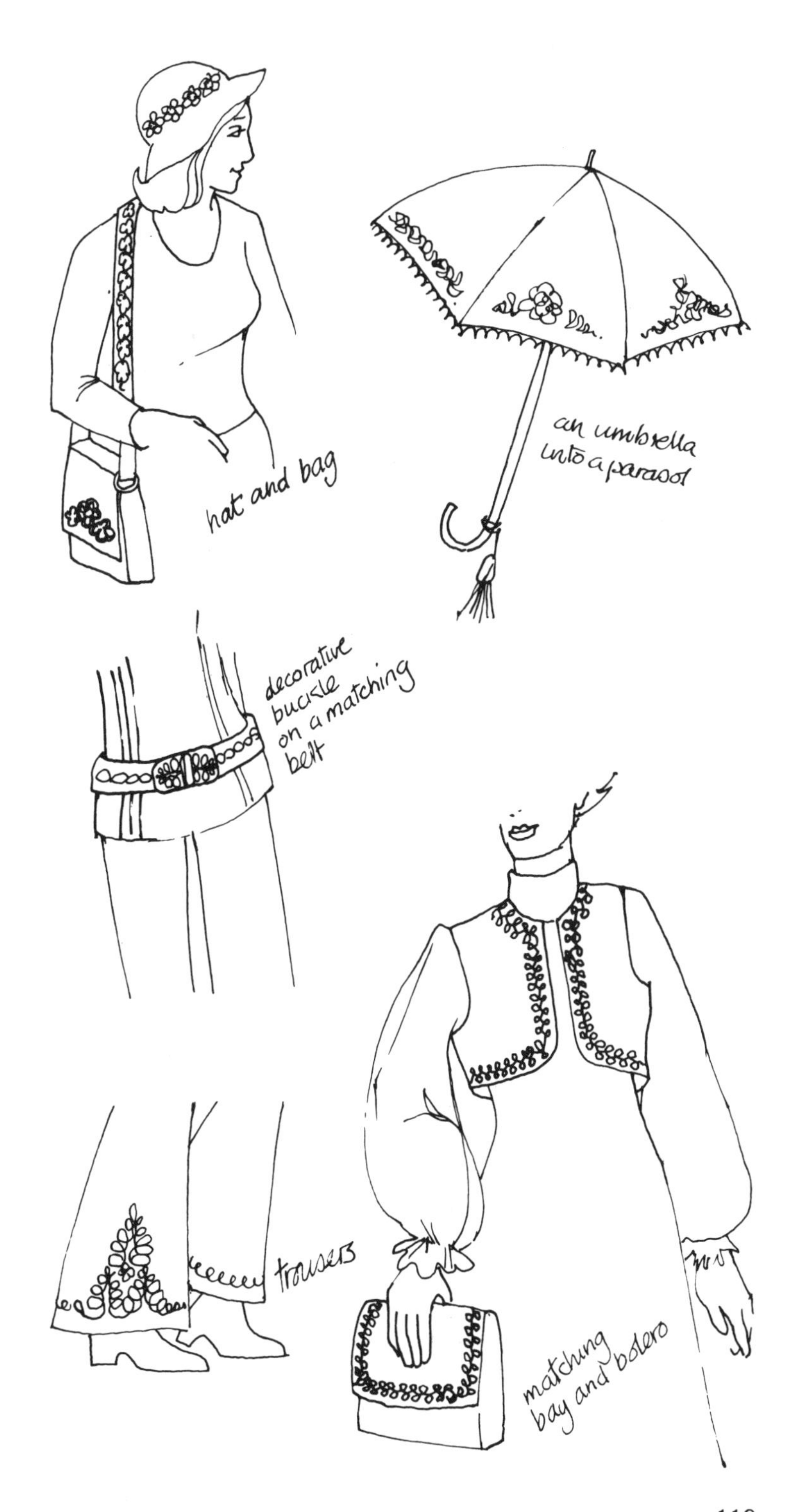
hat and bag
an umbrella
into a parasol
decorative
buckle
on a matching
belt
trousers
matching
bag and bolero